Moving On

Supporting Parents of Children with SEN

Alison Orphan

 David Fulton Publishers

David Fulton Publishers Ltd
The Chiswick Centre, 414 Chiswick High Road, London W4 5TF

www.fultonpublishers.co.uk

First published in Great Britain in 2004 by David Fulton Publishers

Note: The right of Alison Orphan to be identified as the author of
this work has been asserted by her in accordance with the
Copyright, Designs and Patents Act 1988.

David Fulton Publishers is a division of Granada Learning Limited,
part of Granada plc.

British Library Cataloguing in Publication Data
A catalogue record for this book is available from the British
Library.

ISBN 1 84312 113 1

Typeset by RefineCatch Limited, Bungay, Suffolk
Printed and bound in Spain

Contents

Foreword

Parenting is, without doubt, a tough job. As we know an additional challenge like a multiple birth, a child with health issues, a physical or sensory disability or learning difficulty can make that tough job *much* tougher.

Awaiting this manual with excitement, I can't express how chuffed I was to receive and read the final draft.

I think you will agree that Alison has produced something which will actively support and assist parents, carers and professionals. Not only is it studded with facts and gems of insight but there is also a tool box crammed with skills and strategies to learn, use and reflect on in our day-to-day lives as parents of a child with special needs.

What makes this manual particularly important is the ever present voice and experiences of real parents underpinning everything and the empathy, humanity and irreverent humour which are some of Alison's unique gifts as a mum and a colleague.

I hope you enjoy and value this programme as much as we do in Sure Start Newham.

Jenny Deeks
Head of Service, Sure Start Newham
January 2004

Acknowledgements

There are so many people to thank: Jenny Deeks for believing it could be done and believing I could do it; Julie Newman for help and support; Anne Crisp for not only being the most tolerant manager ever but also suggestions and editing; Greg and Jane Smith, Val Davies and Mary Howard for comments and help; all the parents I've interviewed, especially those at Exchange, who are the inspiration and drive behind the book; friends and family who have really been there for me practically, especially Margaret, Hazel, Liz, Lesley, Fi and Dirk; and everyone at David Fulton Publishers, especially Linda. Finally I owe a huge amount of gratitude and love to Si who's walked every step of this book with me, been driven half mad by it and still managed to be encouraging and do all the printing.

This book is dedicated to Carys and Jonathan who turned my world upside down and by doing so made it a far better place.

Introduction

In the UK today, possibly as never before, parenting is fast becoming an almost impossible job. We live in a competitive culture where expectations are ever higher, as compassion seems to be lower and our society is more fragmented and fluid. Parents often do not have the traditional extended family close by to support and help them and while this is true for all parents, for parents of children with special needs it is doubly difficult. Our society is at the very least hesitant about disability and in many cases actively discriminates against it.

In 1999 the Department of Health estimated that there were 549,800 children with special needs under the age of 18 in the UK (Department of Health 1999). Each of those children will have been seen by various professionals, assessed, discussed and have reports written about them. But at the end of the day when the reports are filed away most of the children go home to parents and carers. This book is written with those parents and carers in mind. Families in this situation face many issues that are way beyond what other parents have to deal with. Yet it is recognised by many professionals working in this field that the support they receive is generally inadequate and sometimes non-existent.

As a parent with two children with special needs, I live this unusually challenging parenting experience 24 hours a day, seven days a week. When my children were diagnosed, I looked for and wanted support for the enormous job that seemed to be facing me. I wanted to talk about how I felt and I wanted to process what was happening at home, and work out how to change some things. I also wanted somewhere to go where I was recognised and encouraged as a person. I found very little support. I did meet some lovely people but by and large they were there to work with my son or daughter not with me. The effect of keeping going with little support can be physically and emotionally draining. The effort of coping or trying to cope with daily needs of children with special needs takes its toll. And that's before you add in external pressures such as finding the right sort of services and help for the child and an education that meets their needs. At the same time as looking for support myself, I was facilitating groups for parents as part of my job as a family community worker. I knew from long experience that parenting courses and groups are an excellent way of supporting parents. However, there was little material for parents of children with special needs and what was available tended to be focused on managing children's behaviour rather than the general needs of parents themselves. That was the beginnings of this book: a mixture of what I knew would have helped me as a parent and what I'd observed working with parents.

The book has:

- Eight chapters covering themes affecting parents of children with special needs, such as building up support, communication, dealing with stress and strategies for life. Each of the chapters has two sections: 'The way it is' and 'Moving on'. 'The way it is' considers the reality of lives for parents who have children with special needs and 'Moving on' provides practical ideas that may help.

- A group work manual designed for a parenting support course based on sessions that complement the book's themes.

- A resource directory.

I do not claim to be an expert in the fields of child development or special needs. The edge to what I am writing is that I am a parent who also happens to be an experienced family worker. Therefore this book is for parents and professionals alike. Although a number of academic sources are referred to, the basic thrust of this book is practical. It is intended to be a resource book – something to dip into whenever your particular situation will allow, although if you want to read it from cover to cover you're more than welcome!

The book is also written from my personal experience, so I use 'him' far more than 'her', because Jonathan provides the basis for so much of it; similarly I write as a wife, so more often than not use that context in discussing relationships. Recognising that far greater diversity exists in our society, I would hope that the ideas and principles are valid for everyone.

For the purpose of the book I have a broad definition of disability and special needs. It means a physical, mental or emotional impairment, which has substantial and long-term effects on a child's ability to carry out day-to-day activities. Such an impairment may affect:

- their appearance
- their mind or body

- pain or tiredness
- communication and memory.

Special needs can also mean a difficulty with learning, which means that they cannot access the education available to them. The definition always implies that there is still a person there who has potential in his or her own right.

The material in the book has been informed by three important groups of people. Firstly, a number of parents who have children with special needs, most notably from the long suffering Exchange group from Canning Town in East London and the parents group at Whittingham School in Highams Hill in East London. I've been working with both of these groups and they were kind enough not only to be interviewed but also to act as guinea pigs to try out much of the material within the book. They remain as always an inspiration to me. Secondly, a number of professionals in both education and health who were happy to be interviewed for the book. Professionals can get a very bad press from parents. And yet most of the ones I've dealt with have been a source of strength for me as well as being really committed to my children. In the context of the book many of them have been very generous with their time. Thirdly and last but not least, my family, without whom not one word could have been written. It might be useful at this point to introduce them as they are referred to so much later on! First of all, Simon my husband, referred to throughout as Si. We've struggled together, not always agreeing but somehow managing to stay sane. He is a partner in every way. Then, Carys our nine-year-old daughter, who is currently in mourning over the demise of S Club; artistic, funny, extremely perceptive and in love with her hamster Basil. She is diagnosed as having specific learning difficulties, in her case particularly affected by dyspraxia and dyslexia. And, finally Jonathan, also known as Jono, our six-year-old son, who is passionate about trains, books and cuddling, and is very affectionate, determined and joyful. He is diagnosed as having autistic spectrum disorder with severe learning difficulties.

The recurring theme within the book is the thought that children with special needs, no matter how severe the impairment, are first and foremost children. The process of diagnosis can sometimes confuse and make us forget that. For a time certainly with Jonathan I couldn't see beyond his autism to the fact that he was still a little boy. And, equally as parents we are still primarily parents although often also advocates for our children, nurses and even therapists and teachers.

A long-term study carried out by the Social Policy Research Unit called 'Positively Parents' found, unsurprisingly, that the major motivating factor of the 20 parents with disabled children interviewed, was love for their child (Beresford 1994). The study goes on to make the logical conclusion that if love is the major motivating factor then supporting the parent and child relationship should be the major priority when thinking of supporting families with children who have special needs. So a key issue for me is rediscovering the benefits of having a positive relationship with our children and holding on to that discovery. But to get to that point involves clearing a lot of things out of the way first. Here are some of the issues that we'll look at:

- Practical concerns

  This book starts with a chapter called 'Beginnings' (Chapter 1). This covers the time before, during and after diagnosis. This is often a really difficult time and what parents often need at this stage is practical help. When you're in a crisis there is no time for much reflection. What you want to know is how to get free nappies, how to apply for Disability Living Allowance (DLA) and how to access support. So in Chapter 2 'Building up support' we'll consider building up these practical support systems.

- Belief systems

  Even in those early stages intense feelings are already starting to show themselves. Many parents at this point are working from a position of guilt – 'This must be something I've done wrong.' – and have a very low opinion of their own parenting. What emerges from this are beliefs about ourselves that are simply not true. We'll consider those in the chapters on 'Communication and relationship building' (Chapter 3) and 'Behaviour' (Chapter 4).

- Looking after yourself

  Most parents of children with special needs very quickly become 'carers' rather than people in their own right and looking after themselves is at best very low down their list of priorities. Parenting children like ours is often overwhelming; parents are often very tired, if not exhausted. The chapters on 'Stress' (Chapter 5) and 'Families' (Chapter 7) look at how crucial it is to take care of yourself and your partner in order to have enough resources to do the job of parenting.

- Facing the feelings

  Coming to terms with how you feel, who your children are and how best to meet their needs is a lifetime's journey. Chapter 6 'The emotional journey: facing the feelings' is a beginning in considering the intensity of feelings that parents of children with special needs often feel.

■ Letting go of magic

In our instant society we cast about for something that will cure our kids and sort out our family life. Unfortunately, there are no magic cures but there are problems that can be solved and processes that really help. The chapter on 'Hope' (Chapter 8) looks at problem solving and finding new ways to do things.

When these things are cleared out of the way it's more possible to get to a stage of being hopefully realistic. Realistic about the difficult times that are likely to be ahead. Yet also hopeful because we believe in ourselves as parents again; we understand how important we are to our children and we know we can make a difference.

I hope we also get to the point where we realise simply that we love our children and that we can see them for the joy they bring not just to us, but to others as well. Donald Meyer (1995:25) puts the point really well.

Peering into the bed of a child with a disability in the pre-dawn moonlight can bring tears of unconditional love – love that will not be based on report card performance, scores as a star quarter-back or excellent performances as a respected trial lawyer. This love is for who this person is, for their qualities, their trials, and for the inner strength they must develop to take their place. It is their struggle – we can only hope and help, watch and love.

Beginnings

The way it is

When I was researching this book, I came across an entry in my journal. It was written a few days after Jonathan was diagnosed. Yet it does not mention the diagnosis and how I might have felt about it. I'm obviously feeling pretty bad and yet seem to have no awareness of why that might be the case. No one at the time had told me how the news might affect me emotionally; I had no framework in which to process what was happening.

> ☞ **My story 17.02.00**
>
> I completely lost it today,
> I had about four hours sleep,
> I got up to take Jono to playgroup.
> I knew I was losing it,
> I couldn't find his shoe,
> He wouldn't come when I called him,
> He wouldn't keep still when I was putting his trousers on.
> I shouted at him, I said any minute now he was going to get a smack,
> He looked terrified.
> I said sorry then sat holding his hand crying,
> We were really late for playgroup.
>
> In the afternoon, when I'd picked him up,
> The chasm of the afternoon faced me.
> I felt very frightened.
> I tried to do functional things:
> Fed him, changed him, sang to him, sat with him and watched 'Winnie the Pooh'.
> But still it was only 1.30 p.m. and Jono was bored.
> I didn't know what to do.

'Go to toddler group' I said to myself;
'But I can't' I said back 'When I'm as vulnerable as gossamer',
'I feel if someone breathes on me, I'll just float away'.
I couldn't go out,
I couldn't stay in.
Tried ringing everyone I could think of, no answer.
Finally spoke to Si.
I told him what had happened, it doesn't sound much.
Then I cried, those sobs must have been in me all week.
There are so many more,
He said he'd come home.
I felt foolish, anxious.
I knew underneath he would be angry and stressed,
I felt I should cope but I wasn't,
I was so desperate for someone else to have care over Jono and Carys rather than me.

I feel so guilty about Jono,
I'm so tired.
Where is *all* this anger coming from?
What is going on?

Paths to diagnosis

Whenever diagnosis comes, it is a difficult time. For some it comes at birth, the excitement and anticipation of pregnancy can give way to fear and uncertainty. Sometimes the news is given to parents in the context of ongoing support; someone to talk to who can help you process what you've been told and work out what to do next. Hospitals have their own guidelines of good practice about how parents should be informed about their child's diagnosis. But often, parents are not offered any support. They go home with a small baby, understanding only a little about his condition, feeling alone in the world with no place to go to work out how they feel or what to do to help him. For others, there is a long wait from the time you begin to notice things that concern you to the time it is finally confirmed by medical professionals.

Many parents go through a lot of difficult emotions during this 'waiting period'. When the child looks normal but starts to have problems with social behaviour, discipline and emotions, it can be very confusing. It's very hard not to go down the road there is something you are doing wrong as a parent.

This can be made worse by those around you who may judge you and your child. It is very hard then to keep hold of your own gut instinct.

📖 **Parent's story**

At 18 months I started to notice that he had no sense of danger. Also he was very unsettled, with no eye contact and really slow development. But, it took two years to get him diagnosed. In that time there was a lot of anxiety, fear and confusion.

📖 **Parent's story**

Until he was four, I thought it was all my fault.

📖 **Parent's story**

I used to think there was something wrong but nobody else did. My family thought he was naughty, just being a boy. Some of my friends thought it was me.

For others the process of diagnosis begins when the child starts school. A teacher raises some concerns about the difficulties your child is having in the classroom. An Individual Education Plan (IEP) is introduced and meetings are planned to review it. Your child is put on School Action and becomes one of the pupils in the school on the Special Educational Needs register. A while later at a review meeting, it's decided to refer him to outside agencies to get some specialist help. This means the child is moved up to School Action Plus. For some parents like me the fact that your child might have special needs and difficulties with learning can be a real shock.

☞ My story

I remember in the nursery when the teacher suggested putting Carys on what was then Stage 1 of the Code of Practice, I was absolutely horrified and really resistant to the idea there was anything 'wrong' with her. I think deep down I felt ashamed that I hadn't picked anything up. I look back with a lot of gratitude to that teacher as because of her Carys was in the system early. That meant she was referred to an occupational therapist who diagnosed dyspraxia by the time she was six.

Finally, there may be people reading this who have waited a long time for a diagnosis and are still waiting. As well as feeling in limbo, not able to come to terms what going on, or be able to plan for the future, it is also a really frustrating time for parents. Life seems to revolve around seeing one professional after another but all they give is confusing and vague comments with no diagnosis.

If this is your situation Contact a Family produce a really useful fact-sheet called *Living without a Diagnosis*, there is also a support group called SWAN (Syndromes without a name) which provides a 24 hour helpline (see Resource directory for details).

The diagnosis process

Very often, parents' first port of call is their GP or health visitor. Sometimes this can successfully kick off a referral process either to a consultant at a hospital specialising in your child's likely condition or to a Child Development Centre to see a community paediatrician. This process in itself can be difficult.

However, sometimes, the first person you see can judge you as an overprotective parent or one who isn't coping. Then it can feel very demoralising because you are not being taken seriously.

When you get a response like this, it can be a real setback. It's often taken a lot of effort on our part to go in the first place, to then

📖 Parent's story

I'm fed up telling my son's story. I'm fed up justifying that he needs help; it seems such a big struggle even to get a bit of help.

📖 Parent's story

When the GP first mentioned autism I found it very hard to accept; I blamed myself and my husband.

📖 Parent's story

He started to head butt the walls and laugh and I knew there was something wrong but when I took him to the GP's when he was two, the doctor said I was a depressed parent and gave me antidepressants.

be told we're worrying about nothing can be really tough. Many parents have been struggling with a lot of self-doubt anyway. 'What if it's me?' Now it seems we've had it confirmed by a respected medical professional. It can then be very hard to keep going and try and get the right help for our child.

> **☞ My story**
>
> When I first took Jonathan to my health visitor because I was concerned about his lack of speech, she told me it was because his sister did all his talking for him. It took me two months after that to pluck up enough courage to get him referred to a speech therapist.

> **📖 Parent's story**
>
> Just because all you've got is a feeling, doesn't make you wrong. Sometimes a mother's instincts are so strong they are more reliable than anything a professional can learn.

Many parents who I've interviewed, when looking back on the diagnosis process, have emphasised to me how important it is to believe 'in your gut feelings'. If your gut feeling is that you believe there is something that needs investigating you are probably right. And in the end you will be proved right, so it's important to keep going even when there are setbacks. Sometimes with a hidden disability like Attention Deficit Hyperactivity Disorder (ADHD) it can take a long time to uncover what is really going on and in the process, children are labelled in different ways as having behavioural problems because they're not managing at school. Very often there is an implication that we as parents are not doing our job properly. All of this makes it more important that we listen to our own instincts.

The diagnosis

The moment of being given the news of your child's diagnosis often sticks in your head years later. How we are told and the support we're offered afterwards fundamentally affects our reaction to our child's disability and to professionals for a long time. If you're told sensitively, are given good quality information and offered support immediately then it's possible to process, adjust and move on. But if you experience a medical explanation that neither gives you enough information nor shows regard for how you may be feeling, it can be a very traumatic experience.

My journal entry at the beginning of the chapter is a fairly vivid picture of someone going through trauma. The dictionary definition for such an experience is shock, disturbance, ordeal, suffering and pain. I was experiencing such intense emotions that I was unable to function normally. And yet I had no understanding of what I was going through so I thought it was my fault. At the Child Development Centre a few days earlier, having just been told that our child had a lifelong condition, we were referred on to other services but were offered no immediate support. We were simply given a few leaflets on autism and told we would be seen again in six months time. Then we went home, as if nothing had changed and yet everything had changed. We had no road map to work out where we were; no one had told us how this news might make us feel.

It's worth pausing for a minute, to look at this in a bit more detail. We are all different in the way we react, but there are a number of reasons why the diagnosis may be a disturbing experience.

Parenting moves from private to public domain

In our society the way we care for our children and our family life in general is seen as a private thing. 'It's nobody's business but our own' is a common feeling. The diagnosis process involves very detailed questions being asked about what is going on at home. Although necessary for the professional, it can seem to question our parenting. Alison Cowen, herself the parent of a child with special needs notes: 'Professionals need to be constantly aware of their own assumptions and attitudes about disability' (Cowen 2002: 9).

The sad fact is that questions that need to be asked about home life can sometimes turn into questioning the quality of the parenting the child is receiving. This is particularly true when you have to tell the same story over and over again to a number of different professionals. As parents we are incredibly sensitive to any judgement because at this time many of us are already experiencing a great deal of self-doubt in our ability as parents.

Parents may not receive the help they want

Many parents start the diagnosis process desperate to get concrete help for their child at home and at school. However, very often there is an intense time leading up to a diagnosis with lots of appointments, but energy from professionals goes into the process of diagnosis rather than what to do afterwards. The consequence is that when it's all over parents can feel much worse because we have an expectation that we'll receive something in way of help or ideas. We can feel more alone and more vulnerable than we did before.

 **Parent's story**

It made me glad to know what was wrong with Harry but I felt disappointed because I didn't know how to help him.

You go in with a child and come out with a label

Many professionals in the UK are still dominated in thinking by the Medical Model. It is a view of disability that was developed in the early 20th century by the British Eugenics Society. They were a small but powerful group whose members included Winston Churchill. Essentially, people with disabilities were seen as defective, a burden society could not afford. They were therefore hidden in institutions. Although we like to think we've moved on in this country the reality is that children like Jonathan, who would have been classed as 'severely subnormal', only really started to receive an education in the late 1960s and early 1970s. Attitudes have prevailed which see disability as a problem to be fixed; something wrong that you have to do something about. It's worth saying that we don't just receive these views from professionals; many ordinary members of our community including our family and friends may have the same outlook. However, the fact that medical professionals have this view is important because until recently they had all the power. It has been only a relatively short time since it's been possible to challenge their judgement.

There are a number of implications that can come out of this. These may not be said in words but they are often implied and parents pick them up. For example:

1 Your child, as a person with ordinary everyday needs and interests, can get lost under her disability label. Suddenly it seems someone else – a medical 'expert' – knows more about your child than you do.

2 The diagnosis news is presented as a tragedy; something to feel ashamed about. Your child is faulty with something missing. The implication is that the way the child is now, is bad.

3 The way the prognosis or future for the child is described can be negative. The language used, such as 'This child will never . . .', 'He can't . . .', 'She should not . . .', presents a picture of a life-limiting world with not many options, possibilities or opportunities for you or the child.

4 Disability is the enemy, something to be feared that must be cured. By implication, unless a cure is found, your life as a parent will be sad and hopeless. All your energy as a parent should be around 'curing' rather than living a good life.

So how does this leave us? If we doubted ourselves before, it can often increase our self-doubt. This can lead us to rely too much on professionals. Sometimes we begin to question our own capability as a parent. We whisper to ourselves 'There's not much I can do for him.' Sadly, it can also distance us from our children; we start to see a disability where once we saw a child. For more details on the history of disability see Micheline Mason's book *Incurably Human* (Mason 2000).

The problem of language

Ethnic minority families whose first language is not English can be further held back. You don't just need to understand the basic information about the child's diagnosis but also how his disability is going to affect him on a daily basis. Recent research has shown that although good quality interpreters can make all the difference in the early stages of assessment and diagnosis they are not always available nor is easy to read information in your own language (Chamba *et al.* 1999). Without these crucial services, ethnic minority families, where English is a second language, can feel very isolated very quickly.

Life after diagnosis: the early days

Everybody is different, but many react in the same way feeling the same intense emotions. If you've been fighting for years for a diagnosis your prevailing feeling may be one of relief. However, if your child is young or a baby usual feelings are those of shock, numbness, disbelief, being overwhelmed, hurt, and anger or guilt. One parent described to me that things after diagnosis were like 'Ground Zero'; she couldn't find her way around her life anymore, it was like starting from scratch.

While this is going on internally, externally home life at this point can be chaos. There is much to unravel here. On a very basic level, all the children in the family, brothers and sisters as well as the child with a disability, will be responding to the stress and shock their parents are experiencing. Children do this in a variety of ways but most particularly if they are young and do not really understand what is going on, they use behaviour. They are trying to communicate things that they're not yet able to put into words: such feelings as: 'I'm scared', 'What's happened to Mum and Dad?', 'What is going on here?'

The behaviour that causes parents to seek help for their child with special needs may be even more difficult; this is often the height of sleeplessness, big temper tantrums and real difficulty with boundaries. At this stage we are worn out just holding the line, yet we also have to get our head round understanding our child's condition. Things are further complicated by additional needs which can be hard work to manage, for example visual impairment as well as cerebral palsy, autism and bowel disorder, Down's syndrome and breathing difficulties, dyslexia and dyspraxia.

Home life can be so intensely difficult that it puts a real strain on our relationships with our partners. Often men and women react very differently to a crisis. Both partners will have their own powerful set of emotions to deal with; those emotions will be different and if no support has been offered to talk through these feelings some couples' relationships can start to fragment. Arguments flare up or perhaps couples stop communicating with each other altogether. If there is no outside support it can simply be too much for the relationship to deal with.

Moving on

Here are some practical ideas and strategies that might help.

Dealing with the diagnosis

If you're in that stage of things where either diagnosis is proving to be difficult or you are being referred to a lot of professionals, the following ideas might help:

- Be prepared before the appointment. Sit down, preferably with your partner or a friend, and brainstorm before you go. You've probably waited a while for this appointment, it's important to use it to your child's advantage. Work out the information you want to say about your child and what is happening at home and take some notes. Then, make a list of questions you want to ask. This approach works well whether dealing with health, education and social service professionals.

- If possible request a longer appointment time. If you know you have a lot to say and quite a few questions to ask, it makes sense to plan ahead and ask for longer. Having only 10 or 15 minutes available just puts you under pressure. Normally, as long as this is requested in advance, people are happy to give you more time.

- If you have difficulties understanding English, and here bear in mind how much pressure you will be under, request an interpreter well before the appointment.

- Go with someone, this can really reduce the stress of the day. It's very hard to look after your child, listen to what is being said, ask questions and take notes all at the same time. I can think of some particularly hard days when I have tried to do this with Jonathan; it took me weeks to recover!

- If you're dissatisfied with what your local paediatrician is saying, ask if other options can be explored. This could include a referral to a specialist centre or a specialist paediatrician. Parents do not have a legal right to a second opinion but you can ask for one. If this is the way you would like to go, do some research beforehand. This goes back to following your gut instinct about your child's condition. The Internet can really help here; it is a vital tool for research and opens up information about specialist services.

> ☞ **My story**
>
> Through research on the Internet we became convinced that Jonathan had a bowel disorder as well as autism. This was something the local paediatrician was not picking up. We had to be fairly assertive but we did get a referral to a specialist paediatric consultant and five months later Jonathan was diagnosed as having 'Leaky Gut Syndrome'.

Information

At this stage the more information you can get hold of and understand the better.

The maze of professionals

When Jonathan and Carys were going through the process of diagnosis, one day I worked out that between the two children we were seeing 14 different professionals. At no time had anyone sat down with me and explained clearly what they all did and what all the tests and investigations my children were going through actually meant in practice.

Knowing and understanding 'why' helps reduce stress. It could be that someone has explained all the different roles professionals have in your child's life and what all the checks on your child mean. But if not, there is some information in the Appendix at the end of **Handout 8** Signposts under the heading 'What people do' that should help.

Find out about your child's condition

There are many ways of doing this. I've already mentioned the Internet – an excellent way of gathering information. Requesting written information in your own language from the professionals dealing with your child is also a good idea. Finally, contacting national and local specialist support organisations can really help. This could be your first opportunity to talk to another parent in a similar situation. Again, helpful organisations and websites are listed at the back of the book in the Resource directory section.

Find out what support you are entitled to

The next chapter of the book, 'Building up support' deals with getting the right support for your family from financial to practical concerns. But it is worth saying here that families caring for children with disabilities need support services right from the early days after diagnosis. When you are in shock, it's easy to do what Si and I did and try to go on as normal. One parent in the Exchange group in Canning Town put it well when she said: 'Learn from me, don't do what I did, get support early.'

Be kind to yourself and your family

Thinking back to three years ago, I know things would have been a lot easier for me, Si and the children if I had just been kinder to myself. Very often parents are their own worst enemies and that was certainly true of me. I was a harsh and constant critic of myself throughout this time.

Parents in our situation need a perspective. For most of us this time in our life is a crisis. People don't 'perform' in a crisis, they get through it and survive. We also need to make allowances for the rest of the family: partner, child with special needs, brothers and sisters. They are also often doing the best they can in very difficult circumstances.

Rethinking disability

For many of us, me included, our child is the first experience we've have of disability. So, it comes as a personal shock to discover how disabled people are treated in our society. Over time many parents change their views on special needs and become determined that things will be different for their children. In 1981 at a conference in Singapore a group of disabled people formed themselves as Disabled Peoples International. The basic principle for their organisation was that the suffering caused to a disabled person was in the main the result of how society responded to them. This became known as the 'Social Model of disability' inaugural conference of Disabled Peoples International.

There were a number of implications that became part of this model:

1 Any child with an impairment should be seen for what they can do rather than what they can't. Someone of value who has something to offer. Someone with gifts and abilities that our society needs.

2 Our children are much more than simply the medical label handed to them by professionals. Therefore it is not the professionals who are the real experts here but those who know the child's strengths and needs and understand what the experience of disability is like for that child. The real experts are almost always the child herself and her close family.

3 Society must change and be restructured; there should be inclusion not exclusion for our children. As far as many parents are concerned, inclusion starts with schooling as well as leisure activities such as youth clubs and play schemes. Inclusion is not an easy path for many parents; although things are changing, in parts of the country, the change is slow. The Resource directory lists some organisations that offer support and advice on inclusion and educational issues.

4 Resources must be provided so that our children can access ordinary services. The next chapter 'Building up support' looks more closely at this issue.

5 Community networks and friendships should be set up and nurtured. It's very easy for families of disabled children to become isolated. What we need are networks of people who can support each other.

Rethinking disability is important: not only does it help you to see your child in a different way, it also puts you on the path to building up support, for yourself, your child and the other members of your family. (For more details about the Social Model of disability and information on the inclusion process see Parents for Inclusion, the Inclusion Press and the Centre for Studies on Inclusive Education in the Resource directory.)

Building up support

The way it is

This quote could have been from me as I identify with it so closely. It is actually taken from a parent interviewed for Rita Jordan's (2001: 191) book *Autism with Severe Learning Difficulties*. It shows really well the way it is for parents of children with special needs. We're ordinary people with no choice but to live extraordinary lives. This chapter is about 'Building up support' but before considering ways of getting support some of us have a barrier to cross: we feel guilty about asking for help. This first section considers why our family life can be so different from the lives of other families and thinks about the possibility of new ways forward.

Home life

When I've talked to other parents about their home life, a common response when is 'They don't know the half of it.' In other words people viewing our lives from the outside have no idea of the daily battles we often face just to get through each day. There are so many things that other parents take for granted that are either impossible for us or incredibly complicated. Simple tasks like buying a stamp can become enormously difficult. On top of that are all the extra things we have to do. When you have babies or toddlers you expect to be up half the night, changing nappies and dealing with tantrums. But when the child reaches school age, five, six, seven and beyond, you have a natural expectation that life will get easier. Yet for most of us, it continues as relentless and demanding as it was when they were two. The energy and time needed from us is massive. For each of us it's different. Here are a few examples:

- oxygen-dependent children who need constant monitoring

- children who are awake for long periods at night

- incontinent children who smear faeces

- children who have to be watched all the time because they have no sense of danger

- children who have great difficulties controlling their emotions whether it is anxiety or anger.

Isolation

Very often, having a child with a disability sets the family apart from others. There are many reasons, some outside yourself, some going on internally.

The aftermath of diagnosis

If you're not offered support after diagnosis you can feel fundamentally alone. Part of that is shock, the world goes on as before, people go on as before, yet you're stumbling and struggling to work something out that seems unfathomable. You just want to be with people who understand and they seem hard to find.

Society

When out with their child most parents can experience other people's discomfort: the distance, the averted eye, or the whispered comment. This is true for many of us with disabled children but for those parents whose children have hidden disabilities, whose condition cannot be seen obviously, it can be even harder. Part of these children's condition means that they have difficulties with social behaviour. Thus parents can often have a hard time in public. They can be subject to quite hostile responses like direct disapproving comments and loud tuts. Whatever our situation the effect on us is like a dripping tap; it gradually lowers our self-esteem and can cause us to feel more and more different.

Social exclusion

Parents can feel that they and their child are excluded from all the normal social opportunities that other children and their parents have. The expression that best describes this is social exclusion. It starts young; the number of times I was told that Jonathan couldn't have a crèche place because of 'health and safety' considerations! Even nursery places can be affected by it. There is a parent I know whose child was only allowed to go to nursery for an hour every day when all the other children could stay for two and a half hours. Feeling excluded continues at school; if your child is in a resource provision or special school, special transport picks up children so therefore there is no contact with other parents. You miss that daily contact that all parents enjoy. Connection and contact for parents comes into many social activities that typical children take part in; they are a really easy way to meet up with people and parents often enjoy swimming classes and football training just as much as their children do. But this can feel a whole world away from the experience of parents like us. What happens often is that our children are either stopped from going entirely due to 'health and safety' or they start going and then are asked to leave because of problems with behaviour. This is a situation many parents have successfully fought and changed. However, to move from isolation to a feeling of being connected and able to change things, means building up your support networks.

Practical problems

If you haven't got extended family living nearby who are able to cope with your child or particularly understanding friends, the reality is that it's harder to get babysitters and it takes a lot of energy to do so. This sets a vicious circle into motion: you don't go out because you can't get a babysitter. Eventually people don't invite you out as much.

Ourselves

I know from personal experience that we as parents can isolate ourselves. Much of this is to do with previous bad experiences of going out. It is common among many families that gradually the family hardly ever go out together; one parent will take the brothers and sisters off somewhere, the other parent will stay with the child with special needs. Very often too, parents go out together less and less; the energy of looking for a babysitter can be such hard work that you give up trying. This can be very damaging for everyone. It's really important for all family members to enjoy being together and feel part of a family. Parents crucially need time on their own to talk, to have a laugh or just to drink an uninterrupted cup of coffee. Without this, very little is going into their relationship. It's also negative for the child with special needs, he has fewer and fewer normal experiences and so can get frustrated.

Parents' story

We got it, DLA, first time, which was good and bad. It was good that we got it, but it was confirmation that something was wrong.

(Beresford 1994: 52)

Financial matters

There are many reasons why parents find it hard to apply for disability benefits. For some it means recognising that your child has special needs. Also, the actual process of applying particularly for Disability Living Allowance (DLA) can be very difficult and time consuming because you have to recount the story of your family life in a lot of detail.

However, there is absolutely no doubt that caring for children with special needs costs more money. Parents with disabled children face three times the costs of parents of typical children (Dobson and Middleton 1998).

☞ My story

Below is a list of some of the costs that my husband and myself have incurred in the past few years that are significantly different to typical families' needs:

- special food for a restricted diet (much more expensive);
- redecoration of living room and replacement of carpets in downstairs rooms due to damage caused by Jonathan;
- special education tools and books for Carys;
- transport costs incurred when taking both children to appointments at hospital, opticians, occupational therapists and family therapists;
- hard-wearing (and therefore expensive) toys and resources for Jonathan that are not easily destroyed.

There are many other expenses that families like ourselves incur: often it is more important to keep a car on the road for essential transport; when you have a child who needs constant attention, a cleaner is a good idea; and you tend to go through more clothing and bedding.

It's hard to pay for these things because it's much harder to work if you have a child with special needs. It's really difficult to get childcare even if you can afford it. And there are many appointments to go to especially when the child is younger. Parents are squeezed between health and education professionals who just assume you don't work, and employers who are often not sympathetic to your parental responsibilities. There is new legislation available to working parents of children with special needs but we have yet to see how it will work in practice.

Why is it so hard to ask for help?

How a family deals with having a disabled child can depend on the level of support and understanding they receive within their community. Without support the sense of social isolation can get worse and that increases the chances of what is undoubtedly a stressful situation, becoming a crisis. And yet many of us find it very difficult to ask for help. Logically it is obvious that we need help, so what stops us? Here are some possible reasons:

- Our culture

  We live in a culture where self-reliance is the normal standard; we are supposed to be able to manage on our own. If we need help, even if our need is legitimate, we feel guilt and shame and lesser people for asking.

- Being able to give back in return

  The 'Positively Parents' study showed that the extent to which it was possible to give back in return, influenced how much parents used informal support. This often prevented parents asking for extra help when it was for non-functional issues such as going out for a treat (Beresford 1994: 29).

- Fear

  We fear overburdening family and losing friendships by demanding too much support. We do not want people to feel obliged to look after our child.

- Parent-coping mechanisms

  One way of coping is to just 'get on with it'. Somehow you're surviving a difficult situation. Asking for help can feel like undermining that way of dealing with things. Another way is to have a social or work life that is separate from the child and when you're in that life with those friends you rarely talk about your child.

- Painful emotions

  Shock, grief, anger, whatever it is we're feeling causes us to construct belief systems that stop us asking for help. This includes thoughts such as:

  'I am the only person who has ever felt like this.'

  'This is my responsibility, I should be able to handle it.'

  'Others will not want to hear about my problems; they will have enough of their own.'

- Exhaustion

  Life can be so draining and complicated, our focus as parents can be simply to get through the day with us and our children still in one piece. We often don't have the energy to explain everything. More often than not, you don't say anything or you play down how hard things are.

■ Stigma

Asking for help, especially from statutory support services, can again cause parents to feel as though they are admitting failure.

A new way of being: interdependence

Disability changes a family's life and puts you outside society's normal expectations. Micheline Mason's story in *Incurably Human* (Mason 2000: 64) is a story of finding interdependence. She is a wheelchair user and when she moved into her own flat for the first time she felt she must do everything for herself. So, she cleaned the flat herself by crawling around the floor. People admired her for her 'fierce independence' and thought she would be insulted if they offered help. The problem was it took all her time and energy to do things which took others one tenth of the time and she was not able to do the work she was really skilled at. She got a home help. The story illustrates a really important point.

As parents of children with a disability, normal household tasks take far longer; shopping trips and paying bills are far more complicated. When we try to do everything ourselves, the payback is more isolation and loneliness. The way we feel we have to be is to manage as best we can and cause as little trouble as we can for others. We're still trying to live by the old rules of independence. What Micheline Mason and others are advocating in the Inclusion movement is not that you move to dependence but *interdependence*. With co-operation and teamwork, we can still have control over our lives, live better, more fulfilled lives and have the resources to give back to society. It just makes more sense; human beings are naturally sociable and we gain emotional strength as well as practical support from having people more involved in our lives. And crucially they gain enormously from being involved in our lives.

📖 **Parent's story**

It makes you feel like you're giving up. You feel like you're giving up on your own child. I know it's ridiculous but you do. It's your child, you should be able to cope, he needs you.

(Beresford 1994: 48)

Moving on

When I interviewed parents for this book most of them had very little support for themselves and their families. For many of us building up support is not easy. It can be dependent on a variety of factors most of which are outside of our control:

- Whether our extended family is near enough and then able and willing to help.

- Where we live. Some areas have very good statutory services available that are quick to respond. In others services seem non-existent. Also location makes a difference in terms of how near you are to a support group.

- What our family situation is. Being a single parent or in a relationship will make a difference. If you do have a partner there are still many factors, such as job, personality and approach to parenting, that will affect how much support he or she will give you.

Whatever your situation, it is likely that at some point in your child's growing up you will have to fight for services and support – be that education, health, benefits or social services. Sometimes it will be important to remind yourself that you and your family have the same needs and rights as any other family: for good health, emotional well-being, and good family relationships. It's just that it is more complicated for you to sustain family life therefore there will be times when your family will need more support than others. To build up support we need practical help, emotional resources and a positive relationship with professionals.

Practical support

The 'Positively Parents' study found that actively seeking information about services and rights can help relieve emotional distress (Beresford 1994). Information not only helps us to understand our child's disability and any treatment or therapies available but also puts us in a better position to demand the best level of services.

So where do we start to find information?

Signposting

In the same way as there is real confusion about all the different professionals working with your child and therapies on offer, there is also uncertainty about where to go for services you need. No one seems to tell you. So in the Appendix at the back of the book **Handout 8** Signposts lists where you need to go for everything from special cutlery to special toy libraries. I really want to encourage you to be persistent here; very often it may take a number of phone calls to get what you need and sometimes the agencies themselves are not aware of the services they should provide.

Local knowledge

You can be in an area for a long time without realising a particular service or group exists. It is worth scanning papers, going to local libraries, doing web searches (Contact a Family are very good – for details see the Resource directory) and attending meetings advertised for parents who have children with special needs just to find out what is going on locally. Other parents are often the best source of local information.

Voluntary organisations

These are a great place to gain information, advice and support. They can be set up for specific conditions such as autism, be based around a particular issue such as being a carer, or be more general. They are often more flexible and easier to be in touch with than statutory organisations such as social services. As well as providing information they often organise practical help such as play schemes and have other parents involved with them.

The best way of contacting them is through the local Citizens' Advice Bureau, library or Council for Voluntary Service (CVS). Also the Resource directory at the back of this book has a list of national organisations. Contact them and they will give you their local associations or branches.

Competent babysitters

Having a break is important for any parent, it's just more problematical to arrange when you are the parent of a child with special needs. The National Strategy for Carers was launched in England in 1999. Whether you benefit from this depends on how your local authority has put it into practice. It could mean regular short-term care is available. Also since 2000 the Carers and Disabled Children's Act has entitled parents and carers of disabled children to an assessment of their needs. (For more information see the Resource directory for carers organisations. The Carers UK website is very good.) Again what you get in practice tends to be a postcode lottery.

Most short-term care is given through social services, although some local voluntary agencies also provide it. It might mean your child going away for the weekend or a link worker coming to your house. Speaking as a parent who receives a link worker in my home, it has some definite benefits. This arrangement can be very flexible to suit your changing needs. There are many reasons why you might request this type of help: being very tired, wanting to spend time with your other children and wanting to have time to re-establish identity as a person rather than a parent are important. Significantly, time away from your child can be crucial if you're scared that you are hitting a really rough patch. It could prevent things getting out of hand.

Education support

Two new pieces of legislation (Special Educational Needs and Disability Act 2001 and Education (Special Educational Needs Code of Practice) (England) Order 2001) quite recently came into force and together they explain how information should be gathered about children and how children should be supported in schools. The legislation supports inclusion and it is now harder to treat disabled children less favourably in an educational setting. (For more information on this see the training pack *Making it Work – Removing disability discrimination – Are you ready?* (Stobbs and Rieser 2002) produced in partnership with a number of organisations including the Council for Disabled Children, contact details in the Resource directory.) A more detailed description of the education process (**Handout 5**) and some explanation of the terms used for special needs in the school setting (**Handout 6**) are included in the Appendix at the back of the book.

You should know where to go when you want independent advice, especially when you're unhappy and do not feel your child is receiving the level of support they need.

Most local authorities now have Parent Partnership Services (PPSs). They provide advice and information to parents whose children have special needs. Although they are funded by the local education authority (LEA) they provide an independent service that gives neutral and factual support on the special educational needs (SEN) framework. The idea is to help and support parents play an active and informed role in their child's education. To find out about PPSs contact the special needs section of your LEA. Very often it's really useful to have someone with you at the meetings you're asked to attend, so an Independent Parental Supporter (IPS) can support you by attending meetings, and helping you understand the SEN framework. Such people are either friends, another parent or they will be from a PPS or a voluntary organisation. It is my experience, that PPSs and an IPS can really make a difference. Education can be one of the largest sources of stress for parents of children with special needs; difficulties and conflicts where you don't agree with the professionals about what is best for your child can be very distressing. Having someone to support you through it takes some of the pressure off and makes you feel less alone in the process.

If you remain dissatisfied and unhappy, particularly if the LEA have turned down your request for an assessment or Statement and you want that decision reviewed at an independent tribunal, then there are specialist national organisations who will be able to support you and may be able to represent you. Finally there are a number of publications available to help you. Details of how to order these as well as addresses and websites of useful organisations are listed in the Resource directory.

Financial support

Benefits

We have already noted that bringing up a child with special needs can cost up to three times the cost of raising a typical child. There are millions of pounds worth of benefits that remain unclaimed every year. So if you think you or your child is eligible, claim! For a list of benefits you may be entitled to, see **Handout 7** Benefits in the Appendix at the end of the book. A good place to start is the Benefit Enquiry Line (for contact details, see the Resource directory). This is for people with disabilities and their carers. They give free advice and can send you the benefit forms.

When you receive forms through the post, it's a big temptation to just put them in a drawer somewhere! Benefits, particularly the DLA, have long and complicated forms that require a lot of energy and resources to complete. Sometimes you really need someone with skills and knowledge to help. You can get advice in person from your local Citizens' Advice Bureau, also some local voluntary organisations often have benefit advisers.

If you are not happy with a decision you receive about a benefit, you need to appeal within one month. When you receive the decision by letter, it also gives you details on how to appeal.

Direct payments

Direct payments are new for parents and carers but I think may be a creative way to help us. You will be visited by a social worker, he or she will then talk to you about the situation at home and what sort of support you need. Once this is done, you can ask for a direct payment so you can buy the services yourself.

Family Fund Trust

When you begin to receive DLA, you will often receive a leaflet about the Family Fund Trust (see the Resource directory for details).

They have an excellent website, which not only gives you details on whether your family is eligible but also has information on a whole range of practical issues from bedding to holidays. The Trust cannot help you with anything that is the responsibility of someone else. So it can't for example provide respite or window locks (social services) or nappies or wheel chairs (health authority). The range of things it can help with though never ceases to amaze me, from washing machines to driving lessons, as long as they are related to the care of your child.

Once you've sent your application in, one of the Trust visitors will come to your home and decide how the Trust might be able to help. You can apply once a year to the Family Fund.

Transport

Getting around with a child with special needs can be really hard work – whether it's the struggle with a wheelchair or the child like Jono who just likes lying down on roads! There are a number of ways to tackle this problem:

Motability

The DLA has a mobility component: if your child receives the higher rate, you can receive Motability by signing over your mobility component to a scheme operator for three years. This is to help to lease or buy a car outright depending on what scheme you choose. It also covers you for insurance and maintenance costs. You need to have three years on your DLA claim remaining in order to qualify. In the Resource directory there is an excellent website for the Family Fund Trust that gives you all the details.

Local schemes

Many areas have local schemes such as Shop mobility and Dial-a-bus to help with transport for disabled people. To find out what is available, contact the Public Transport Officer at your local authority.

Hospital

If you are on a low income, you can get help with fares to hospital for treatment and for visiting your child in hospital.

Road tax

This is often overlooked, but if your child gets the higher rate mobility component of DLA you can receive an exemption on your road tax. Contact the Benefit Enquiry Line (see Resource directory) for details.

Safety harnesses

Parents are often asking me for seatbelts that their child can't get out of when they have outgrown a child seat. Crelling (for details see Resource directory) is a very helpful firm which specialises in safety harnesses for disabled children.

Family Fund

The Family Fund may be able to help pay for driving lessons and also, in some cases, travel expenses if your child gets a lower mobility component or nothing at all.

Publications

The Royal Association for Disability and Rehabilitation (RADAR) publish a good publication called *Door to Door* which gives detailed information on help with transport (for details see Resource directory).

Equipment and adaptations

Good quality equipment and helpful adaptations can really reduce stress at home. It can make it easier for you to care for your child and make the child's life happier and more comfortable.

Equipment

It is surprising what is available free. Refer to **Handout 8** Signposts in the Appendix to find out where to go. For the most part, whatever equipment is needed, your child will need an assessment by either an occupational therapist or a physiotherapist. This will be set either through the hospital or social services department. When it comes to equipment, it's really important not to forget yourself. As they grow older, children with physical disabilities can be very demanding on their parents. Make sure you get proper advice about lifting and possibly some equipment to help. There are some excellent organisations in the Resource directory that give more information and provide equipment.

Adaptations

Adaptations seem to be another maze that families who have children with a disability have to negotiate. Adaptations can range from small-scale work, such as window locks, to large-scale building projects, such as extensions on your house. Disabled Facilities Grants are available to cover this and these come under the Housing Grants, Construction and Regeneration Act 1996. The grants are there to help with the cost of adaptations to housing for disabled people including children to make their lives as independent as possible. However, the issue is that these grants are means tested on the parents' joint income, so often you have to make a big contribution. You need to give yourself a lot of time for decisions on what you can have and who will pay for what. To get started, contact social services who will send an occupational therapist to visit you at home. The Muscular Dystrophy Campaign have published an *Adaptations Manual* to help families work through this difficult area (for details see Resource directory). RADAR will also advise you if getting a Disabled Facilities Grant is proving tough.

Housing

Parents' story

In Exchange, two families have been successfully rehoused in the past two years because of their children with special needs. Both children in question were autistic and living in flats. As well as drawing a network of people together who would help them, both families wrote a long and detailed explanation about how their child's disability was affected in the place where they lived. They included such examples as Grace, the five-year-old girl who was terrified of using the lift, so that whenever she did she would attack people, or seven-year-old Samuel, who did not sleep at night and regularly disturbed the neighbours on all sides.

Sometimes, no matter how many adaptations you make, your housing is just completely inappropriate for your child. In this case, you need to consider moving. 'Oh great,' I hear you say, 'add another stress to my many why won't you?' Taking a long-term view though, overcrowding and unsuitable housing makes bringing up a child with special needs far harder (Oldman and Beresford 1998). If you're a council tenant or live in rented property, it's important to persuade your local housing office that you need to be rehoused. This is not an easy task but it is not impossible either. You need to find people who will help you and campaign on your behalf: local voluntary organisations, GP, social worker, your child's school, a local councillor and even your MP may help. Part of it is building up awareness about what it's like to live with your child in the housing you currently live in, something that people in authority who make these decisions often have a really vague idea about.

Emotional support

Find someone who will really listen to you

Being fully listened to is special. Every human being needs it. However, parents of children with special needs need it more than most, particularly in the early days. Confiding our pain and feelings of stress while going through a crisis greatly increase physical and mental health, whereas holding onto it means that our chances of suffering from all manner of health problems grows. Emotional distress also lessens our ability to work through our problems, whereas speaking about feelings untangles them and clears our minds to think. To do this though we need listeners: people we can trust.

What we want are people who:

- will hear our story and connect with us;
- can handle our pain and stress;
- don't jump in with lots of advice and many words;
- are there for us and who are not just drawing the attention back to themselves.

Support groups

Not everyone finds it useful to belong to a support group but for those who do it is important to find one that offers the kind of support that best meets your needs. Some support groups are condition specific, often local offshoots of national associations such as the National Autistic Society, while others are more general.

Fundamentally support groups provide understanding; you don't have to worry about having to give lengthy explanations as people know where you're coming from. And at a time when we often feel very isolated they also provide perspective: 'I am not the only one in this situation.' You can let off steam and have a moan without people thinking any worse of you. There are often older parents present who can let you know what might follow and provide positive but realistic ideas about the future. You give as well as receive and that makes you feel stronger and more self-confident. And, most importantly, you laugh about everyday situations gaining as Naseef (2001: 218) says: 'a hearty sense of comedy in everyday life.'

☞ **My story**

The idea of comedy rings true in my mind. There are days at Exchange where we are just crying with laughter. Like the time when we discovered that four of us had pliers in the bathroom to turn on the taps because our kids had flooded the bathroom so many times that the taps had broken.

As we've already noted support groups are also a good place for getting and exchanging information about local resources, schooling, benefits and practical tips.

Informal support

As most humans are sociable it makes sense that we would get support and strength from relationships. When we're thinking about building up our network of support, it's important to look at what is already there. The 'Positively Parents' study (Beresford 1994: 16) noted some important groups where parents receive a lot of support.

📖 **Parents' story**

The comments below are from parents of the Exchange support group in Canning Town, East London.

What we like about Exchange:

- Bouncing ideas
- Off loading
- Two-hour rest
- 'It's about me'
- Help with situations
- People in the same place as me
- Friendly faces
- Information
- Getting things done
- It brings you out of yourself
- Gives you the will to carry on
- Gives you hope
- Fun
- 'I know it's OK to be all night'
- Sharing ideas
- The way the group links up with other organisations
- People
- 'I wouldn't know half what I know if I didn't go to Exchange.'

Partners

Partners are critical. It seems especially important that the parent who did most of the care for the child felt supported by their partner. This is often the most important relationship. If that support is there, it makes a real difference. Without it parents could feel really alone.

Brothers and sisters

If brothers and sisters are older than the disabled child, they often could provide real help and support.

Extended family

Grandparents seem to be the main source of support when it came to the extended family. This is partly due to normal expectations on both sides. Parents felt it was more reasonable to ask grandparents; the grandparents want and expect to help.

Friendships

Most parents have maintained friendships with people they had known prior to birth of their child with special needs. Friendships can be so important, not just because they can provide practical and emotional support but because with friends you can have a life outside of being a parent. You can be a person, have fun and have a laugh. There are different degrees of friendship: some may become our listeners, some will be really good at offering practical support but others will be the ones you go to for a good night out, also really important.

Coming to terms with our new life, means a gradual shift in all these relationships. If you look at the ideas of interdependence that we've already considered, it may mean asking some of these people for help for the first time. It might mean accepting the fact that you're not as able to help out and be there for others as you once were. In the shift come some amazing compensations. It often brings you closer to people than you were before and people gain so much from helping you.

> ☞ **My story**
>
> Last year, I was desperate to find a child minder for Jono one night a week after school. The search seemed impossible until a friend offered. I felt really anxious that this would be a real burden for her. But what I discovered was not only does Jono have a really good time, but her husband comes home from work early because he enjoys being with Jono. Our friendship with them has really deepened now thanks to our son.

Relationships with professionals

I think positive relationships with professionals are a really important part of building up support. However, it's not always an easy path. We need to take a closer look at why these relationships with professionals are so important, the problems that get in the way and ways we can work through them.

Our children

No matter how difficult early experiences are with professionals, our children need us to have good working relationships with the people whose job it is to help them. In 2003, we are facing the reality that there are too few resources available for most families who have children with a disability. Relationships with respect and understanding on both sides are going to help your child get the services he needs.

Parents are seen as legal partners with professionals

Recent legislation means that parents are increasingly seen as legal partners with professionals. The new Education SEN Code of Practice for example measures the success of any school's Special Needs policy as to how much parents and professionals work in partnership. It actually states that parents' unique strengths, knowledge and experience are to be recognised as important, and that their 'wishes perspectives and feelings' have to be taken into account when deciding on a child's future. This situation is also true in Health & Social Services. If we can have these rights in law, it stands to reason that if we can get good working relationships things are going to work out better.

> **See:**
>
> SEN Code of Practice (DfES 2001) (Para 6 & Para 2(2))
> The Children Act (1989)
> The Children (Scotland) Act (1995)
> The NHS & Community Care Act (1990)
> The Children (Northern Ireland) Order (1995)
> Health & Personal Social Services (Northern Ireland) Order (1991)

Barriers

The problem with building these relationships is that there are many barriers. No matter what the law states some professionals are reluctant to be anything other than 'benevolent dictators' (Coyne Cutler 1984: 247). However, we as parents have our responsibilities too. This is particularly true if our early experiences of the period leading up to diagnosis were negative. If we're not careful this can stick in our memories so that we start to believe this about all professionals for all time. So here are some myths about professionals which act as large barriers to building up real relationships. I've included some quotations from my interviews with professionals.

> ☞ **Professional's story**
>
> The hardest thing in the parent–professional relationship is that parents expect you to know everything and rescue them. We are just as human as they are.

1. Professionals can fix all your problems

This quote came from an early years practitioner, and reflects the situation that often exists between parents and professionals, especially at the beginning. There are many reasons for this. The culture common in our society based on the Medical Model means that we expect professionals to be like God: have all the answers and be able to fix everything. When we see professionals at this point most of us don't want to be there. Our relationship with them as Naseef (2001) notes is based on 'desperation and necessity'. In our heads for many of us it's going something like this: 'just fix his problem and get me out of here' (Naseef 2001). Some professionals add to this by reassuring us that they do have all the answers. Although professionals can have a great deal of in-depth knowledge it is based on assumptions that could and should be questioned. They can be emotionally attached to a theory that may or may not be right in all cases. The best sort of professionals are the ones who know this; those who give time and space to parents and really listen to their issues and concerns. Whatever your experience with a professional though, it's really important to remember that the professional does not always know best.

📖 Parent's story

Until he was four, I thought it was all my fault. I felt as though I've let Andrew down, I listened to professionals too much, I took everything as gospel. I've learnt to listen to myself more now. I respect myself.

2. Professionals have all the power

What follows on from this is the belief that professionals have all the power and there is nothing we can do to change this. This affects many things. It means if we have a gut instinct that comes through our own daily observations of our child we let what professionals say override our gut instinct. So, we allow decisions to be made about our children that deep down instinctively we know aren't going to work. One parent I interviewed said she had learnt from this experience.

3. We have to perform for professionals

A lot of parents like me think we have to be on our best behaviour for professionals. Do our performance of 'I'm a wonderful parent and I'm coping really well.' One professional summed it up really well when she said: 'Some people will clean the toilet when they know you're coming round.' There can be absolute chaos in your house, battling with no sleep, mystifying behaviour, destruction of furniture and a child in a lot of pain and yet when the professional visits we clean the toilet or vacuum or clean the kitchen floor! What is that about because I do it as much as anyone else? I think it's back to fear. We're full of doubt about our ability as parents. We believe that we are going to be blamed for what is going on. So we paper over the cracks and smile, when what we really feel like doing is screaming. What a professional needs is the real story about what is going on at home. We don't help our child or ourselves if we don't tell the truth, however painful.

4. When it goes wrong it's the professionals' fault

In the early days especially there is a lot of anger around. The diagnosis process as well as being traumatic can also be a trigger point to anger. If parents have a bad experience, particularly when the expectation is that professionals will 'fix our problem', our anger can be huge. Lack of trust can build up, so the next professional we see we go in there ready to be angry with them; we're expecting them to let us down. The truth is that sometimes we are really let down by incompetence or lack of care on the part of individual people, but often it is lack of resources that are the real enemy. There can be a lot of blame going round: professionals can blame the families and families can blame the professional. When actually the real picture is that there is a lack of resources to meet needs.

5. Professionals don't care

Sometimes professionals do not appear to care; they are cold and clinical rather than understanding and they let us down by not doing what they say they'll do. But my observation, as both a professional and a parent, is that while there are always professionals who aren't that bothered and don't really care, there are many who do and who are struggling very hard to get the right services for our families. Some observations are that professionals:

- have huge caseloads and pressures to meet deadlines. Sometimes they are just not able to get things done as quickly as you need them doing.

- can be really affected by working with our children. They also have their own emotions: from excitement to distress to anger that support can't be provided for the child.

- may appear not to care when actually they just don't understand the enormity of our situation as parents. They are often not experienced, trained or supervised to deal with families as a unit. So much of the focus appears to be on the child and there often seems to be a lack of awareness of the intensity of the emotions parents are experiencing, often being asked to repeat their story for the tenth time. One of the issues I hope will be tackled in the future is this ignorance on the part of professionals. Partnerships with parents seem to be the new way of working in many organisations. I hope that means that parents will have more opportunity to speak about their experiences and professionals will make more time to listen.

- and parents often disagree and yet they have much in common. This is especially true of those people who work with our children everyday or weekly: teachers, learning support assistants (LSAs), transport escorts, speech therapists and after-school workers. They are also rewarded and encouraged by our children's successes. They too feel sad, unsure of their ability and frustrated when there are problems in behaviour or learning. And in a typical day they often go through very similar emotions to ours when dealing with our child.

☞ My story

When I watch some of the professionals who work with Jono I often feel very emotional. I see their commitment that goes over and above a job and often I feel a deep attachment to them because they really have got his best interests at heart.

Speaking as a professional for a moment, I know that if I'm noticed in what I do by parents it keeps me going, but if people just expect me to deliver it's much harder to carry on.

Ways of moving forward

Moving forward comes when both parents and professionals respect and understand each other. This is a long process and I'm only really providing some places to start from. There seems to me to be four key issues here for parents. Parents need to:

1 Learn to respect their own experience and expertise

We do so much that we're not aware of. In a sense this book is about identifying our strengths, for example

- we manage difficult stressful situations often using only our own resources;
- we have a 24 hours 7 days-a-week knowledge of our child;
- we have an interest and commitment in our child that no professional could equal.

Once we understand that we're experts on our own children the next key issue is to learn how to communicate what our family wants and needs.

2 Learn how to communicate effectively what our family wants and needs

So often, we assume that professionals, because they're professionals, understand what is going on at home – well most of the time they're not going to, unless we tell them. And the way we tell them is also important. However rightfully frustrated we are, shouting, screaming and threatening generally causes professionals to feel defensive, to say the least.

3 Recognise the strengths that professionals can bring

Professionals, whether teachers or health professionals like speech therapists, are trained to observe and to overcome your child's barriers to learning. Also they often have a broad knowledge about your child's condition from their experience of many different children. This can all really help your child.

4 Cultivate relationships with professionals who listen

No matter who they are, listening professionals who give you time are allies for you and your child. They can help in many ways, some of which are unexpected.

When a relationship is working

A positive relationship between parents and professionals can be hugely valuable. You can meet some beautiful people working with your children. Here are some signs that a relationship is working:

- This person is really committed to my child.
- This person listens and is a source of emotional support.
- This person sees beyond my child's difficult behaviour and values my child.
- This person makes me feel I have important things to say.

■ This person is supportive to me and doesn't add to my guilt and pressure.

Such people often counteract difficult experiences that you might be having elsewhere.

☞   **My story**

At the same time as Jonathan's diagnosis, he was attending a mainstream nursery. When I came to pick him up, they never complained if I was late (even though I often was), they always told me something positive about what he'd done that day (even though later I would find that he'd stuck his head down the toilet or tried to climb out the window) and they always made a point of asking how I was. As you can imagine I never wanted to leave.

Communication and relationship building

The way it is

When I first focused on communication I automatically thought of speech. Therefore the whole issue was focused on Jonathan. He has only a few words and for the majority of the time babbles. By implication, there was no problem with Carys because you can't stop her talking. For years, this was my focus. I would go to bed and dream of holding conversations with Jono. When no speech came the pain in the silences between us was terrible. Slowly, partly through researching this book and partly through observing my son, I've realised that there is far more to communication than words.

I have to say I felt very daunted when I came to write this chapter. Communication is an incredibly complicated subject. However, I do know that it's the lack and the breakdown of communication that causes parents so much pain. It's pain that I've lived with myself. It's from that place of struggling to understand that this chapter is written. Many children with special needs have speech and language disorders as part of their condition; some are mild like Carys, others are severe like Jonathan. All cause difficulties for their parents.

As usual, this chapter begins with this section on 'The way it is'. This is divided into two parts: 'Communication and feelings' and 'Understanding what is going on'. The 'Moving on' section is also divided into two parts: 'Ways of being' considers how we can deal with our own emotions and beliefs and 'Ways forward' looks at practical strategies.

Communication and feelings

Our society makes a number of assumptions about communication that go very deep in the way we view other human beings. These assumptions include the following:

- Communication is about words

  We live in a society that is based on words. How you speak, the way you speak and what you say are all incredibly important. We judge our relationships by the word test:

  'She's not speaking to me.'

  'He never tells me he loves me.'

  So strong is our belief in the necessity of words that without it we wonder how a relationship is possible.

- When someone speaks, he understands what is being said to him

  Automatically we assume that if a person can speak our language he or she can understand what we say to them.

- When I speak to someone he understands all the things I don't say from the expression on my face, my tone of voice, and what I do with my body while I'm speaking

  We expect a person to understand all these things at the same time as understanding the words we're using. Very often, we let people know how we're feeling not through using words but in all the other more subtle ways just mentioned. So I can say something quite neutral like: 'This bus is late,' but leave the person I'm speaking to completely sure that I'm very angry without mentioning anger.

How this affects parents and children

Although we think of communication as words, the assumptions we often make show that communication is complex and multi-layered. When children don't communicate or don't respond to our communication it causes complicated and intense reactions within us.

When a child doesn't speak and responds very little to you

Most human beings are born with a desire to be connected to each other. That desire is at its strongest between parent and child. We communicate with the child, the child communicates with us; connection occurs and a beautiful relationship begins. So what happens when the child doesn't speak and doesn't seem to respond when you speak to him?

Sometimes our feelings can go really deep and we can start to question whether a relationship exists between the child and ourselves.

Our child's lack of communication also causes us very early on to question ourselves. It's common for parents to feel that it's some

Parent's story

I don't know if Charlie actually knows who I am: he has no words.

thing they have done wrong; to blame themselves. And even to take it further than that and question their abilities as a parent.

Many children are late at speaking for a variety of reasons. It could be a hearing impairment or a learning difficulty. Although these children may not speak for a really long time, they do often have a desire to communicate. This desire is what professionals call 'communicative intent'; it is at the root of communication. Children on the autistic spectrum, however, often do not speak and have no wish to even respond to you. And it is this apparent lack of desire to communicate which some people call being 'in their own little world' that some parents find so difficult. Sometimes you can start to feel that you have no significance to the child. Slowly what can creep in is a belief that you are inadequate as a parent. If that lack of communication is also accompanied by a lot of difficult behaviour your feelings as a parent can become really negative.

> ## ☞ My story
>
> When Jonathan was three and had virtually no speech, little eye contact and hardly any desire to engage with me, I remember detaching myself from him. It seemed as if I was going through the motions of being his mother: caring for him well and yet not present. I realise now that is what happened because whenever I tried to play or engage with him, he would push me away or walk off. At that moment, I felt so rejected and hurt and so useless as a mother; detachment numbed the pain. My detachment often made me quite robotic in my responses to Jonathan and made Jonathan's non-communication worse, propelling him further into his own little world. So, without meaning to, we started a negative spiral between us.

We will all react in different ways. Some like me will feel a bit like a robot, just going through the motions with this child. A common feeling linked with being detached is depression. And the trouble with depression, as I've discovered, is it's a kind of blank feeling – you don't feel anything. Others feel frustrated and angry and try many ways to get the child to respond. However, often this ends with the child continuing not to speak or respond but also developing some difficult behaviour, such as biting or kicking. Either way, as a parent it doesn't seem a very good deal: little positive feedback from our child and behaviour as if we don't exist, or demanding behaviour when we are treated like a punch bag. So all the time our confidence slips away and all the time we feel less and less sure that we're doing anything right as a parent.

> ## 📖 Parent's story
>
> When Tayo was little I felt guilty that he continued to be detached; I felt that it was because of the way I had been in the first two months of his life.

When a child does speak but still doesn't communicate or understand what is being said

Parents who have children who do speak and yet still have communication difficulties will ruefully tell you that those longed for words aren't everything. Meaningful communication depends not just on gaining language. There are a myriad of different communication difficulties. Here are just a few.

■ Children who repeat everything you say

This is called echolalia. Words are repeated with little understanding of meaning.

■ Children who just talk at you rather than to you

Here a child just talks endlessly fairly repetitively and obsessively about her pet subject. It's not a conversation because it doesn't build on what someone has just said, in fact it doesn't appear that the child is listening at all.

■ Children who have difficulty processing language especially instructions or long conversations

In a very similar way to no speech at all, a child who speaks but does not communicate or understand what is being said causes intense reactions in parents. This is particularly true if, like us, you didn't understand that your child had any communication difficulties.

> Carys was extremely verbal from a very early age so for a really long time we couldn't see that there could be a problem with communication. And yet, when she came home from school, when we asked a fairly simple question the whole house would erupt with shouting from Carys and from us. There seemed to be no reason for it. And, because it happened frequently, it did begin to have that same spiralling effect on our relationship with her that non-communication had had on my relationship with Jonathan. The reality was that after a day at school, she was having difficulties processing what we were saying. As we didn't understand, we felt things that other parents I've interviewed have also experienced:

– Anger and exasperation with the child

We were not seeing this as a communication problem but as disruptive behaviour; each time it happened our anger increased. But even if you do understand what is going on, having a child repeat what you say all day or lecture you on the finer points of signalling on East Anglian Railways can lead you to distraction.

📖 Parent's story

Attempting to have a conversation with him sometimes makes me want to scream. I say 'James do you want some apple or orange juice?', he says, 'Juice'. So I try again, 'Apple or orange?', he says 'apple or orange'. In the end I just give him orange juice.

📖 Parent's story

He asks the same question over and over again every two minutes.

– Confusion and madness

Asking a simple question and getting a volcanic response at first causes confusion but after a while has you starting to question your sanity. Was I really speaking English? Did I ask too much of her?

– Fear

A lot of unresolved conflict in any family produces fear. I began to live with a feeling of dread: I knew what was going to happen, it was so predictable. My reaction was fairly predictable too. I attempted to pacify her and as that generally didn't work I would slip into feeling inadequate as a parent again.

In both cases, my children's behaviour was as a result of communication difficulties. But in both cases my relationship with them became very negative and I started to question my own abilities as a parent. Other parents have spoken of similar reactions, with many emotions mentioned from exasperation to dislike of their child to despair.

Understanding what is going on

To begin to move forward, we need to understand what is going on. It is only then that we see it is the child's disability that is causing the communication problems, not our parenting. It is at that point that we can begin to turn the relationship around.

There are reasons why our children do not respond in the way we would expect, but to find out what is going on we need to take a journey all the way back to babyhood. We need to look at the normal development of communication in babies and toddlers. There has been some important research done studying the relationship especially between mothers and babies. This is a good starting point so we can build up a picture of what usually happens from a parent's eye view at each stage of a child's early life and what can happen for a child with special needs. It gives us insight into not just why our children might have difficulties in communication but also why we, as parents, often struggle in our relationship with them. As a working example, I've looked at what happened to Jonathan and how this affected how I felt. It is worth saying that problems can occur at any stage. The information in this next section has come from Brazelton and Cramer (1990), Hobson (1995), Trevarthen *et al.* (1996) and the excellent explanation of how communication works by Jordan (2001: 6, 24–29).

Stage 1: Beginnings

Eye contact

With a tiny baby, a parent is set up ready to play. The parent looks at the baby, the baby gives eye contact. It is the baby's eye contact that is the trigger to keep the interaction going. This is the beginning of communication. The parent responds to eye contact (mostly with a 'coo' or baby-talk).

Turn taking

The next stage even with very young babies is that the parent will pause and expect something back from the baby. Whatever that response is, be it a burp or a look, it is responded with enthusiasm. Showing the baby that his contribution has meaning and value.

Emotion sharing

The baby is crying, the parent looks down and smiles, baby smiles back. Babies have an inbuilt reaction to mirror certain expressions they see on people's faces. When we smile our facial muscles release body chemicals, which make us feel happy. The baby learns that smiling makes him feel happy. The parent also feels good. It is this sharing of emotions that bonds parent and child together. Whenever it happens the baby learns a bit more about the experience of emotions.

Cause and effect

The parent will also copy the baby's facial expression, making it bigger on her face and the baby will then respond to this.

What is the baby learning?

He is learning;

- how to take a turn in a human 'conversation'.
- that eye contact and an expectant facial expression are the cues for his 'turn'.
- what it feels like to share emotions with another person: the beginning of empathy.
- self-awareness: he has an effect on the world.
- to make an emotional connection: 'When I do this it makes me happy.'
- to develop the ability to understand and begin to control what he does.
- to develop his memory: 'I remember my own part in what just happened.'

All this rich learning about communication from early interactions is something that most parents with babies just take for granted.

What can happen to children with special needs

It used to be thought that it was all the parent's responsibility to make these interactions happen. The implication being that if a parent and child didn't bond, it was the parent's 'fault', but research has shown that the child's response is vital to the parent.

When Jonathan was a baby he only ever gave me fleeting eye contact; he would stare at reflections but hardly ever at me. As I've been pondering on this I've realised that this was perhaps the most painful part of being Jonathan's parent. Eye contact is such a basic human response and when as a parent you don't receive it, all sorts of reactions happen inside. I felt chronically rejected and I also felt on a very deep level that Jonathan didn't need me. He seemed content and happy without interaction from me, as long as I fed and changed him. So taking Jonathan and me through the different steps and with the help of lots of experts, let's see if we can discover what happened.

☞ My story

- Jonathan does not give the eye contact trigger: I keep trying to get it but after a while give up.

- I feel rejected and importantly I begin to expect less from my relationship with Jonathan, looking after him becomes a little bit more of a chore and less of a pleasure.

- My energy level goes down when I'm with him and I start to switch off. I would find myself reading a newspaper when I was with him, something I would never have done with my daughter.

- I talk and play less with Jonathan. I mentioned before how robotic I became, but the thing I remember was the silence. He was rarely looking or making noises and I didn't talk.

- Jonathan begins to find interactions with me even less rewarding. I am very blank and uninteresting.

- I withdraw; that was when the detachment started. Looking after Jonathan becomes my duty rather than my joy.

- I begin to believe this is my fault: it's because I'm a useless mother. If it is my fault then I dare not let other people know, I must pretend that everything is all right.

- Some babies at this point start to show behaviour difficulties, often loud and frequent crying and problems in being comforted. Jonathan did none of these things but he did stop sleeping.

All of this began with a biological impairment in Jonathan: his inability to give me eye contact. I remained completely unaware of this. As he became an older baby and then a toddler other things necessary for communication were also not happening. All I noticed was that he wasn't saying many words.

With Jonathan problems started very early on but for other children problems start as older babies and toddlers.

Stage 2: Older babies

Joint regard and shared attention

When a baby of about six months has an object, for example a red ball, held in front of him, he will look at it. Not only that, but he also instinctively knows that this is something Mum and I look at together. The professionals call this an object of 'joint regard'.

At about 12 months, the baby himself will hold up an object, so the adult present can join in and look at it with him. This is called 'shared attention'. By this age he is also moving from tuneful babble to speech-like sounds and often some recognisable words, so objects may now be named.

What does the baby learn from this?

- He learns to concentrate on the same thing as his parent.

- He hears the word 'ball' and sees a red shiny thing.

- He learns what pointing means; this is a way of showing something to someone else.

- When parent and baby look at something together he begins to understand what words mean: 'OK, I get it now that red shiny thing is a ball!'

What can happen

- Eye contact comes into play again here; to look at something your parent shows you, you have to have sustained eye contact. Without eye contact or just fleeting eye contact, joint regard is not possible.

- Many toddlers with special needs have difficulty concentrating and while this is not on its own a reason for communication difficulties it doesn't help.

- Some toddlers with special needs, especially those on the autistic spectrum, observe things differently to their parents. The parent says 'This is a red ball,' meaning the colour of the ball is red. The child looks at the ball and is attracted by the shiny surface; he then thinks 'shiny surface means red'. If a toddler makes out things differently, this is obviously going to have a significant effect on his language and his understanding of the world around him.

Stage 3: Young toddlers

Social and shared play

Toddlers learn so much through playing with each other. There are so many opportunities for learning and trying out what you've learnt. At this stage, between one and two years, they are saying a lot more words and starting to put them together in phrases and sentences. They also understand more of what is being said to them; first of all 'no' and then simple commands like, 'shoes on'.

What does the toddler learn?

- The effect he has on others; through this he learns how to work out what others might want from him.

- He begins to learn how to have conversations through the experience of turn taking.

- He experiences emotions, gains more understanding of them and begins to put names to them, for example 'This is how it feels to be sad.' He plays at being 'Mummy' and 'Daddy' and 'teacher' and 'pupil' and through this he works out what those people do and the right word for them. He begins to learn and understand how to behave with other people, for example politeness and sharing.

What can happen

- For many reasons children with special needs often play on their own and because of this miss out on all of these learning opportunities.

- Importantly, they don't gain an understanding of what is going on for other people; they don't understand what they are doing or feeling. They don't learn how their actions might affect others.

- They don't learn how they feel and they don't have words for those feelings.

- They don't understand or learn the language of play, which is really the social language of how to get along with others.

- Even when they do play alongside other children, often there are difficulties for them to process what is going on around them.

Stage 4: Older toddlers and school age children

Language

Older toddlers, between their second and third birthdays are saying sentences and recounting simple stories. They are also beginning to understand ideas such as 'bigger' and 'smaller' and they can process more than one item of information at a time. By the time they reach school age they've learnt the rules of a two-way conversation; how you need to listen and wait, understand the cues to speaking and know what's OK to say socially. They can understand abstract concepts and begin to make sense of double meanings in language.

To get to this stage is not just about learning how to talk and use words. There are other things you need to do, for example you need to:

- understand what is being said to you;

- be able to process long streams of words, that come in conversations, instructions or questions;

- be able to understand facial expressions, tone of voice, body postures and gestures because they often add to or change what is being said.

What can happen

- Not understanding what is being said causes Jonathan all sorts of problems now he is six: people are much less tolerant of a burly looking six-year-old ignoring a request than they were when he was three.

- Echolalia can occur: words are repeated parrot-fashion with little understanding of meaning. This can lead parents to think their child has more advanced language skills than they actually have.

- Language can be used repetitively; it doesn't build on what someone has just said, it doesn't relate to the conversation and its purpose can be to block out the other person.

- Long streams of words that occur in normal conversations, or commonly in a classroom situation where instructions are given and questions asked, are difficult to process creating a 'log-jam' effect in the child's brain.

- Gestures, facial expressions and tone change the meaning of words. For the child with special needs this interferes with their understanding of what is actually being said.

- Language is often understood literally; sarcasm and metaphors are completely baffling for some children with special needs. The way we use English is so full of things we don't actually mean that it's no wonder some children are incredibly confused. For example, phrases such as:

'Wipe your feet on the mat,' – so a child takes their shoes and socks off and then gets into trouble.

'Can you bring that book to me?' – a child says 'no' and is told off for being cheeky.

■ Children with special needs can have problems sequencing words such as 'before', 'after', 'yesterday' or 'tomorrow' and can find it difficult to find the right word.

■ They can find it hard to stay 'on-track' in a conversation and may skip from one topic to another, often missing the 'big picture' of what is being said.

Moving on

Ways of being

Most parents have a desire for an enjoyable relationship with their child, which makes parents and child happy. We've seen how a child's communication difficulties can really get in the way of such a relationship. I'm not an expert on communication, nor would I be able to recommend a particular technique, but it seems to me that the most important thing is to make that bond between parent and child work. Why? – because everything flows from this:

- Research has shown that a good healthy relationship between parent and child does so much for any child (Greenspan and Wieder 1998). It encourages their development in lots of different ways. I would argue that having fun with your child, enjoying times of comfort and pleasure does brilliant if not wonderful things for parents too.

- The effect on both parent and child is an increase in confidence and contentment.

- This is where acceptance, understanding and forgiveness will happen.

Making this relationship work starts within us and is a difficult process. We love our children but we can also feel some difficult uncomfortable feelings: things are not working out as we expected they would. When this happens, for whatever reason, we are often stunned and at a loss of what to do. Our reaction can in many cases make the situation worse.

Being honest about feelings

- Admit how you feel

  The first step must be to be really honest and authentic about how we feel when our child does not respond in the way we expect. That's hard, in fact of all the things to consider about communication it is the most difficult. It's a brave commitment to be honest. When you've been able to admit how you are feeling the next step is to try not to feel guilty.

- Try not to feel guilty about how you feel

  As I was researching for the book it was really helpful to discover that the feelings I had about Jonathan and Carys were extremely common. A number of parents who agreed to be interviewed for the book mention similar feelings and also the guilt. The fact is we're human beings and these feelings are normal.

■ Work out where our feelings go

Anger and pain can get displaced. It depends on our different personalities how we deal with things, and whether our feelings go inward or outward.

– *Inward* Some people self-blame, pushing anger inside. That way leads to depression but it also leads to beliefs such as: 'I can't do this I am a really hopeless parent.' This is a position you can easily get stuck in.

– *Outward* Others push anger outside and load it onto the person, in this case the child, who is seen as causing our pain. A belief system is developed that goes something like: 'This child is ruining my life.' This is an equally stuck position; it doesn't really go anywhere and it can make us and our child feel awful.

Look at our style of communication

The way we speak to our children is incredibly important. When we open our mouths what comes out is not just words, but feelings and attitudes sometimes that we weren't even aware of. To focus on building up a healthy relationship with our children we do need to look at the way we relate to them.

> **Parent's story**
>
> When we get in, after he's misbehaved, I shout at him and feel so guilty.

When I broach this subject in parent's groups, it's often difficult. Most parents, including me have felt guilty about the way they've spoken to their children at some point or other. Sometimes, though especially with parents of children with special needs, I'm met with anger. The feeling is, it's such a struggle to bring these children up can you blame us for losing it? Yet this is not about blame. I'm well aware that parenting our children is a tall order and also many families have other issues to deal with too, such as illness, depression, alcoholic partners, unemployment to name but a few. However, speaking as someone who has lost it with her children, I know that it does not feel good and afterwards I always regret what I said. So, let's consider some negative patterns of communication and where they might come from. For this section I'm indebted to *How to Talk so Kids will Listen and Listen so Kids will Talk* by Faber and Mazlish (2001), an excellent book on this subject.

Negative patterns of communication

■ Not listening

There are a variety of ways we don't listen to our children. With non-speaking children it might be ignoring their sounds and gestures as 'attention seeking' when they're actually trying to tell us something. It might be not noticing important things that are going on for them, such as their sadness. With children who speak we hear, but don't listen in a number of subtle ways. When they're trying to tell us something, we can immediately jump in with advice, lots of questions or defence of the other person. The scenario that comes to mind is picking a child up from school and finding out she's been in trouble (it's hard to stay quiet and listen then). The other thing that we do often is deny a child's feelings. Again, think of a child coming out of school, in trouble and angry with her teacher:

Child: 'Mum, I really hate my teacher.'

Mum: 'No you don't, you're just having a bad day.'

■ Critical speech

Underlying this sort of speech are ideas about the child that start: 'He's doing that to get at me,'; 'She always does this wrong.' If we use language like 'You are stupid,' or 'You're always late,' we are likely to be blaming or accusing them of something, giving them a label, comparing them with others, threatening them, lecturing them or being sarcastic.

■ Non-reaction

This is similar to the robotic reaction I found myself doing when Jono was little. It seems whatever the children do, you don't react. You might be there physically but your real presence isn't; you've withdrawn and switched off. This can lead you to behave in a number of ways: you may not react to fairly wild behaviour all day and then scream and shout when your son spills his orange juice over tea; or you might make vague comments to them that they neither understand nor react to.

■ Over-protective

This style of communication shows itself in continual anxious comments to our children. There are a lot of 'nos' and 'don'ts' involved: 'Don't do that, you'll hurt yourself,' or 'No, don't carry it yourself, you'll spill it.' It's often quite patronising to the children concerned and may lead parents to talk on behalf of their children. Underlying it is a great deal of anxiety and fear that our children are not going to cope without us continually intervening.

Where do these styles of communication come from?

The main reason for communicating this way is our own unhappiness. That shows itself in different ways: anger, anxiety, detachment, exasperation, but deep down we often feel defeated and desperately tired. We've already begun to look at the importance of admitting to our own feelings but it's worth saying that unhappiness eats away at our reserves and can take all our drive, interest and warmth away. When we feel like this it's really easy to focus on what your child is doing wrong but it's often because we feel really unhappy about our own lives that we see our children as worse than they really are. Communicating this way is also sometimes a learnt behaviour: 'This is the way my parents spoke to me.' But as Faber and Mazlish (2001: 233) comment 'We want to break the cycle of unhelpful talk that has been handed down from generation to generation.'

What does this type of communication do?

■ It sets off a negative spiral in our children

When we relate to our children out of our own sadness, fear or anger they respond quickly to it. It doesn't matter what the level of their disability is, they still pick up what's going on underneath. Children like Jonathan may not understand all the words but they hear acceptance and react to criticism. What can occur is a vicious circle that can be seen clearly in the case of Jonathan and myself. A depressed parent feels more depressed by having a child with special needs, especially one with difficult behaviour who in turn is more difficult through having a depressed parent.

■ It sets children up for failure

Our negative comments, attitudes and tones of voice have a habit of becoming self-fulfilling prophecies for our children. They are already struggling to get by the best way they can. Put-downs or distance from their parents makes that struggle all the more difficult.

Why is relating positively to our children so important?

■ Our children need someone who understands them

Children who have communication difficulties desperately need their parents to take the time to understand, figure out and accept their messages.

■ Our children often have a tough time in the world

Most of our self-esteem and acceptance of who we are comes from the responses we receive from the important people in our lives (Tessler 1995). Our children already have problems with self-esteem: feeling unsupported and not encouraged at school, having their difficulties misunderstood, feeling isolated and often being the victims of bullying and teasing. Their behaviour can be misunderstood as rude or insensitive and their physical difficulties can result in them feeling demoralised and frustrated.

The way we speak to our children can make them feel better about themselves and provide a safe place at home to develop. Then, they can get out in the real world, build friendships and get involved in activities without fear of failure or ridicule.

- **The way we relate to our children is crucial to their progress**

Very often in my life, I come across parents of children with disabilities who are looking for 'the answer', the key element that is going to change things for their children. They're prepared to part with a lot of money to find that vital therapy or get their child in the right school. All these things are important as I've seen with my own children. However, I think we don't have to go looking for the most important thing, it's already there; positively relating to our children can begin to change everything for them and us. When researching the book I came across this quote that, although referring to dyslexic children, could refer to any child with special needs: 'Very little can be done for these children that will be effective and long lasting until they learn to believe in themselves and value their own self-worthiness' (Tessler 1995). It is we as parents, who are able to give children the vital self-belief they need.

Beliefs and attitudes that help communication

To be able to relate in a positive way to our children, we need to have in place a number of attitudes and beliefs about them and us. We need to find a way where we can:

- **feel good about ourselves**

This is where we have to start dealing with our own unhappiness and starting to believe in ourselves again. This is a theme that I return to again and again. Yet it is so true. To care for our children, we have to look after ourselves, our own needs and recognise the important reasons why we sometimes feel terrible.

- **express feeling without doing damage**

Living the life with Carys and Jono, I know there are days when I feel exhausted, angry and afraid; a very stressful life seems to the norm for parents in my position. It's what we choose to do with those feelings that determine whether we do damage to ourselves, our children or our partner.

- have a compassionate attitude to our child

  No matter how many communication techniques we learn, where we are coming from inside makes all the difference.

- have a respectful attitude for a child's struggle

  I don't think our society is very good at respecting children, especially children like ours who have to struggle to do what others take for granted. It's really important that we respect them.

- enjoy our child, rediscovering how delightful they can be

  There will be hollow laughs when you read this. Delightful she says, you try being at my house at 4 a.m. in the morning. This is a challenge for many of us and yet to relate positively to them we need to rediscover what makes our children so great. Sometimes in order to enjoy them again, we need to let go of the attitude that says I need to rescue and save you.

- have an open attitude that wants to give and respond

  I've reached points with both of my children where I've been so tired and angry that I've felt closed towards them. To communicate positively, we need to feel open to them; to be willing to give. Sometimes getting there means looking after our own needs first.

- have an attitude of acceptance and understanding

  It's hard to accept yourself and not feel guilty. No parent is perfect and every parent makes mistakes. However, your child needs *you*, not some perfect icon.

  Acceptance also means starting to take a different view of your child. It means beginning to make sense of the difficulties and limitations he or she might have with communication, and also rediscovering the unique individual your child is. Robert Naseef (2001: 77) says: 'The child with a disability or illness is first of all a child; the disability is secondary.' The point is, if they are first of all a child, you don't have to be an expert in communication techniques to have a wonderful relationship with them, you just have to be their mum or dad. The interesting thing is that when you and your child focus on having fun and enjoying each other's company, communication seems to happen more naturally anyway.

Principles that will help

Start thinking of communication as more than words

As we have seen, communication is crucial but it is far wider than simply speaking. Finding a way of communication will help our children with their behaviour and learning because it gives them more control and helps them to feel less frustrated.

I'm writing this particularly with those of you who have children with little or no speech in mind. When we focus on what comes out of the child's mouth we miss the big picture. I think I spent a lot of time with Jonathan waiting for words that never came, in the process I missed a lot. I missed the fact that he communicated in many other ways. Sometimes we're listening so hard for words, we don't hear what our children are actually saying.

☞ **My story**

A while ago I was picking Jonathan up from his after-school club. As I strapped him into the back of the car, he said his car noise. This is a noise he'd been saying for about six months. It was just one of Jonathan's noises, a background to every car journey. I had never really listened to it. That day I said it to myself and then said it back to him. I was saying, 'brum, brum'. For six months Jonathan had been getting into a car and saying 'brum, brum' and none of us had noticed.

Time, space and silence

I'm not very good with silence. Before Jonathan started school, there was lots of it and I hated it. I wanted words from Jono and because they didn't come I filled it with noise – the radio, music, long phone calls to friends. Carys also suffered from my inability to be silent. I would pick her up from school and ask her tons of questions about her day. One day she got really angry with me and wisely said I was asking too many questions and her brain couldn't cope and would I please shut up.

I've realised that my children and many other children with special needs need time, space and silence to really communicate. There are lots of different reasons for it. Some need time to process what you're saying to them. Others need time to process where they are and to think what they're going to do next.

We as parents also need that time and space. Parenting any child is not an instant business and this is definitely true of these children. Our society is not very good at waiting and often as parents neither are we. When we ask a question or give an instruction we're all too quick to jump in and do it for them anyway, rather than waiting 20 or 30 seconds and seeing what happens. Waiting has some other benefits too. When children are being insistent about something, a silent pause on your side gives you time to process and work out what to do. Going at their pace and being willing to wait for long periods is well worth it. When I'm not asking questions and let my daughter be, I notice more about how Carys is when she comes out of school and when she's ready she'll tell me how her day was.

Ways forward

This section provides ideas and strategies to help develop positive communication. It is split into three parts: general ideas that might be helpful for all children, ideas for children who use language and ideas for children who communicate in other ways.

General ideas

Listening

Real listening is not just hearing; it is giving someone your full attention. What children want is your presence; they want to know that you're there for them. Children just know when you are totally present and they also know when you're faking it. At the stage of telling you something they're not looking for a lot of words. For children with communication difficulties words are a barrier. So listening is about watching and observing what they do; intensely felt feelings and difficulties often come through behaviour. So to listen involves having an open mind; trying to hear the message behind the behaviour they are displaying. It's remembering respect; often children are only trying to look after themselves in the best way they know, in a world that is confusing and difficult to live in.

Listening is also about looking for and taking into account their feelings. You show any child you're listening by simply giving their feelings a name; all feelings can be accepted, some actions have to be limited.

With children with special needs, listening needs to be creative. Sometimes children feel very confused: they know they feel bad but don't know why, they don't really know what they like or dislike and find it hard to make choices. Micheline Mason (2000: 76) gives some less obvious ways you might listen to a child with special needs:

- Go for a walk and notice what captures a child's interest;
- Watch the activities they choose and then create opportunities for that person;
- Hold a person when they cry.

Listening means being there and being there means you're more creative, more fun and more available; children love it.

Christine Mayer (O'Brien *et al.* date) wrote a poem that expresses the whole essence of listening to children with disabilities beautifully:

If you are going to work with me

You have to listen to me

And you can't just listen with your ears,

Because it will go to your head too fast

If you listen slow,

With your whole body,

Some of what I say

Will enter your heart.

Avoid escalation

It doesn't matter how little language they use or whether they never stop talking. It's the easiest thing in the world to find yourself in a verbal conflict with your children. It makes me laugh to think that it's possible to have a row with Jono, but it is.

☞ My story

There's not much language involved but boy are we both angry. Picture the scene: it's 6.30 a.m., Jono is up and raring to go; I, on the other hand, am barely alive. He's hungry so, being a logical child, he hands me a packet of crisps. I say 'no'. I'm not really watching him as I'm making him his breakfast. He then goes to the freezer and finds an ice-lolly. I say 'no' again. He's now getting really frustrated so before I can stop him, he climbs into a cupboard and gets a jar of sweet and sour sauce and hands it to me. I say 'no' again. By now he's making his angry crying noise and I'm stressed and hassled, but fortunately his breakfast is ready which he takes reluctantly. I look at the clock its 6.40 a.m. but I feel as though I've just been through three rounds of a wrestling match.

This happens to me particularly at points in the day when I'm really tired. But I know that letting things escalate like that does neither Jono nor me any good. The signs that things are getting out of hand are when I start saying 'no' a lot. There are many things that can help: planning in advance and giving him full attention are both good strategies. Whatever I choose to do is always better than allowing things to escalate.

The same is also true of Carys. With her it's more likely to be arguments that go on and on with lots of shouting. Often midway through the row, both Carys and myself have forgotten what the original problem was in the first place. It's better to look for a way of calming the situation down than apply ever-increasing force, which is your only other choice. When things are on a more even keel return back to the original issue and deal with it then.

Praise and encouragement

I think praise and encouragement might be the parents' secret weapon. This is not about being fluffy and over the top; it's about noticing them. The key is about praising the *effort* not the outcome. Sometimes children like ours have to make huge efforts, which no one else really notices, but we, the parents, do and they deserve comment. We have the advantage of knowing our children. Also, our children don't necessarily achieve conventionally, such as 'A' grades in maths, but they do many great things. It's about stepping back and appreciating those things too. When our children face so much in our society that is discouraging and difficult, I don't think it's possible to over-encourage.

Sometimes, especially when we ourselves are feeling discouraged, it's very difficult to see anything good that our child is doing, but there will always be something, however small. Often children get things half right and we're often tempted to criticise the bit they haven't done. However, if you work from the point of view that when you see it, praise it, they're much more likely to do it again.

Following the child's lead

When we spend time with our children often at the back of our minds we have something we want them to do; be that their homework or cleaning their teeth. What came through time and time again when I was researching for the book was that if you want to improve communication with your child let go of what you want to do and follow their lead. Many of the therapies for encouraging communication have this as a basic principle.

We tend to think of parenting as 'being in control', following the child's lead means the opposite. You do what they want to do, your time is theirs and there is nothing better for improving a relationship than this. It's not just about giving them time, it's about doing things their way. You might think, as I did, that the thing to do with cars is race them and say 'brum', not line them up for hours, but when Jono plays cars that's what we do. It's also showing interest and enthusiasm in what they like to do, which I know isn't always easy. However, if you take a long-term view the results in terms of your relationship with the child, your child's confidence and often their improved communication skills are well worth it.

To look further into this, particularly for ways in which this approach can encourage communication, see **Handout 11** Communication alternatives in the Appendix at the back of the book which mentions some therapies that may help.

Understanding emotions

To understand their place in the world, all children need to understand emotions and how those emotions affect others. Children with communication difficulties need that understanding more than most. The world can feel very confusing and scary for them and that can raise a lot of difficult emotions. They have problems reading other people and predicting how their actions are going to affect other people.

Children need help with:

- working out feelings and being able to name them. ('OK, so that hot feeling in my tummy and my face going red – that is anger.')

- connecting what they do with how they feel. ('I just hit Carlton because I'm angry.')

- stopping and thinking first, working out what's going on rather than just lashing out. ('I'm angry because he took my truck.')

- guessing what will happen when they do or say something. ('If I hit Carlton again, he'll hit me.')

- learning to read signs other people show. ('Carlton looks really sad.')

- seeing a situation from the other person's perspective. ('Carlton hasn't got his own truck.')

- learning to wait for what they want. ('I'll wait till he's finished playing with it.')

Professionals call understanding these things, 'emotional intelligence' or 'emotional literacy'. My own personal theory is that this type of intelligence is as important as academic intelligence. It makes it possible for you to control your emotions and get on with people – crucial skills for independent living. There are lots of specialist programmes for children with special needs about social skills and emotions. But it is we as parents that can make a fundamental difference in the way we speak and listen to them.

Ideas for children who use language

Clarity

As parents we need to really think about what we say. We need to be clear and not give too much information at once.

Many children with communication difficulties have problems in doing two things at once; too much information means you're asking them to do something *and* listen to what you're saying. They can also have difficulties in thinking and planning ahead and they often have little idea of time. So, rather than asking him to go upstairs put his socks on, clean his teeth and bring his PE kit down and finding him upstairs half an hour later having done nothing except put on one sock, give one instruction at a time.

Here are some helpful points:

■ Don't assume that your child understands; always explain clearly and check back to see if they have.

■ Give out no more than one or two instructions at a time.

■ Break information or questions down into bite-sized chunks.

■ If the child does not respond, follow it up with action rather than words – take them to what you want them to do.

The way we speak to our children

It is important to think about the way we speak to our children. Points to consider are:

■ How we describe things

Describing things in a way that they understand makes children feel safer: they know where they stand and don't feel so lost. Good things to do are:

– Describe what you see and what you expect of them.

– Talk about how you feel.

– Give them space; they need plenty of time to process information.

■ How we deal with questions

The way we deal with questions is important. Don't ask too many questions and when they ask one, don't rush to answer it. As much as possible let the child answer for himself to encourage problem solving. The process of answering a question is often as important as the answer itself.

■ How we use different language

It is possible to say the same thing in a different way and get an entirely different reaction. Good ways of using different language are as follows:

– A good use of words for describing situations is to use '*I feel*' then say how you feel, '*when*' then say what happens '*because*' then say why it affected you.

- If you want to encourage problem solving and feel your child is able to do that, you might say *'What are we going to do about it?'*

- Other questions that might encourage the child to describe what's going on and solve their own problems are *'What could you do differently?'* or *'How did that happen?'*

- When noticing their feeling, a good way of tuning in is to say *'I can see that . . .'* or *'That sounds like . . .'* and then describe the feeling.

- When praising, follow the same process of describing, that is what you see and how you feel. Be creative and put the emphasis on them, *'You must be so proud of yourself,'* is a good one.

Trouble shooting communication

When your child doesn't reply or do what you have asked, ask yourself:

- Does my question make sense in terms of the child's age or ability?

- Can some practical changes be made to make this request easier to do?

- Am I so focused on asking her to do things that I don't have enough just 'be together' time?

- Is it possible to think laterally about this issue?

- I see this as important, he doesn't, can we do the same thing in a different way and reach a compromise?

Ideas for children who communicate in other ways

In this section again I am indebted to the work of Rita Jordan on communication in her book *Autism with Severe Learning Difficulties* (2001: 39, 53–5, 62).

Keep it simple

Children with communication difficulties need simple language. As you have probably gathered I'm one of these people who will always use 50 words when 10 will do. My children do not appreciate this and I've had to learn to be different. For children like Jonathan, who understand very little language, key words and phrases that are readily understood are good, such as 'sit down', 'bath-time' and 'cuddle'. I've learnt a lot from professionals who work with Jonathan about accompanying these with physical gestures, like putting my hand on the chair when I want him to sit down but also using something as a visual prompt to remind him. That might be the actual object, such as his trunks if he's going swimming or a visual card system like PECS (Picture Exchange Communication System) (see Resource directory for contract details). At Jonathan's pace, Si and myself at home and staff at school can increase the amount of language we use. Simplifying language does not mean not talking to the child but it does mean thinking about what you say.

> ☞ **My story**
>
> Jono has taught me so much about what it's possible to communicate with very few words. When he puts his head on my lap, sighs and says 'Ma, Ma' and settles down for a big cuddle, I don't just hear Mummy. I hear: 'Mummy I am content and I like being here.'

Speech systems and early intervention therapies

If a child has no speech, we must give the child a way of communicating as soon as possible. Visual systems are the most effective. Ruth Marchant and Ro Gordon (2001) in their handbook to accompany their video, *Two-way Street* said, 'Imagine then if everyone ignored you when you spoke or consistently misunderstood what you said. Imagine if people do things to you, for you without paying any attention to what you say, to what you need or feel.' Everyone has a right to a method of communication that works for them. As parents we tend to feel that if our child understands speech he does not need a system with symbols and cards. However, even if the child can understand speech, that does not mean he will have the language to express speech; the use of a card or signing system might prompt speech.

Something to communicate about

We have needs and desires and we are aware that we have them. Some children with disabilities have needs and desires but they may not be aware that they have them. Our job is to build up self-awareness for children of what they want and then help them communicate. If there is little communication at all an effective way to start is to copy the child's noises or actions. The Options Institute in the USA have developed a programme called Son-Rise and they call this sort of copying, 'joining'. It seems to be an effective way to begin the process. For details of this and other therapies that encourage self-awareness and communication, see **Handout 11** Communication alternatives in the Appendix at the back of the book.

Acting dumb rather than anticipating

I'm sure you know the scene as well as I do: Jono wants something, he drags me across the room to get it. I feel like a cross between a robot and his third arm. As parents we learn to anticipate, to get the drink out before he asks, because we don't want to be dragged halfway across the room or we think: 'If I don't give him this now, he will have a screaming tantrum.' Thus, things are just how he wants them and Jono has no need to use words or any other speech system because his mother is always available.

So here's a radical suggestion and one bound to cause alarm: rather than giving them what they want all the time because you know every cry and every gesture, start acting dumb. Let them know calmly and in an unstressed way that if they used words or a communication system, you would know what they wanted. So he cries for a biscuit and you know what he wants but you act slowly and confused. Does he want ketchup? A drink? The message is, 'I'm trying but I'm not sure want you want.' But if they use a word or a communication method, act fast and name the word. This way, the child will see that words or a communication system are the easiest way of getting what they want.

Celebrating communication with enthusiasm

> **📖 Parent's story**
>
> When you get a response it's very fulfilling. When my son first looked around for his sister, and when he then saw her and his face lit up.

Every attempt at communication is a major step forward, celebrate what you get and don't take anything for granted. Your reaction is really important to your child. It's a huge effort for them to hold hands or give us eye contact – don't let it go unmissed. The more that you respond to the slightest cue enthusiastically the more chance there will be more. And when I say respond, I'm not thinking dull monotone voice here, sparkle and celebrate; make communication interesting.

Trouble shooting communication

> **📖 Parent's story**
>
> It's not just words that are important – when Samuel waved goodbye for the first time, I felt so happy. I thought:
> 'He waved to the doctor. He actually waved back!'

What can we do as parents? We can:

- Think about what you say to your child. Do you take it for granted that they understand the same as you?
- Give very clear instructions of what the child is actually to do, for example, 'look at me'.
- 'Join' the child to find out why they're doing what they're doing.
- Be a detective – look for clues.
- Be imaginative and sensitive – feel your way in to start the process of communicating.

Afterthought

As I was finishing this chapter, two things happened that have been good to reflect on. One was spending three-quarters of an hour with Jonathan where he gave me almost continuous eye contact. The other was having had a particularly interesting screaming encounter with Carys that was followed a few minutes later when I went upstairs to find her drawing pictures about why she was angry and what her feelings were. This does not mean that there aren't days when Jonathan is still completely in his own world or that Carys still does not have massive emotions to deal with. It's just that children never stay still, they are always developing and growing; communication can get worse but also it can get better.

4 Behaviour

The way it is

For most parents with children with disabilities, dealing with difficult behaviour is one of the most challenging aspects of caring for their child. Behaviour is often extreme, often in the realm of 'I can't believe she just did that.' The stress can be overwhelming. Often you can get stuck just coping day to day; there can be very little time to think beyond what is actually happening.

Their behaviour can be disturbing and sometimes completely mystifying. Like most parents I reacted to my children's behaviour by wanting to control it. The fact that I seemed powerless to change anything caused me to feel angry and frustrated: I felt as though deep down they were deliberately trying to hurt me. And, I was very motivated by what others thought of me. We live in a society where your parenting is judged on how well you control your children.

I know that I'm not the only parent who's felt like this. Behaviour that is intensely difficult to deal with is very stressful and causes many of us to start believing things about our children and ourselves that are not true. The truth is that most of the time children are not deliberately trying to get at us or ruin our lives. In fact most of us have incredible abilities to manage in often very hard circumstances.

This chapter attempts to unravel the behaviour of children with special needs from the point of view of a parent. The first section, 'The way it is', looks at the range of behaviours we have to deal with and the sort of effects it has on us as parents. The second section, 'Moving on' is divided into two parts: 'Ways of being' and 'Ideas and strategies'. 'Ways of being' takes a fresh look at what is going on for us internally and how we can find attitudes and beliefs that really help our children. 'Ideas and strategies' includes a general section for all children and a section that covers specific ideas for children with different disabilities.

The effects of difficult behaviour

Emotions

Children's behaviour generally seems to bring out some fairly intense emotions in parents. For parents with children with special needs the emotions you feel can be as extreme as the behaviours themselves: rage and intense anger at one end to helplessness and despair at the other. It's very tiring and confusing and often we as parents feel we are to blame. This is particularly true of parents of children who have either received a late diagnosis or none at all. Often they have been told by professionals and family alike that it's their fault. Comments like: 'If he were my child I'd be stricter', or 'Do you suffer from depression?' only add to the self-doubt. With both of my children we were fortunate in getting clear early diagnosis and this helped us considerably to get to grips with what was going on.

The cost

The cost is enormous for many parents. It can be really physically demanding; you have to manage the aggression, the lack of sleep and clearing up afterwards. It's also mentally tiring trying to work out what's going on and how to solve or at least manage the behaviour. You would have to be superhuman for this not to drive you to the edge from time to time. However, the killer is how it can make you feel emotionally. Most children touch their parents in extraordinary ways but parenting a child with special needs can challenge your view of yourself as a parent. When you thought about being a parent it was not meant to be like this and your child was not supposed to behave like this.

> **📖 Parent's story**
>
> He doesn't sleep; he goes to bed at 12 and wakes at 5.

> **📖 Parent's story**
>
> I detach myself because if I feel something today, it will happen again tomorrow and the next day.

👉 My story

The worst time for me still is the middle of the night. I've been asleep for maybe two or three hours and I hear him on the baby monitor. My body is crying out, 'stay in bed, get a bit more sleep'. But already his babble is turning into a giggle; I can hear him bouncing on the bed. If I leave it much longer he'll start his happy screaming and that will wake his sister and half the neighbours in our street. So I rush upstairs, my eyes still half shut and I'm greeted by the bright glare of the bedroom light. He's always pleased to see me, but he is ready to play and I want us to lie down and go to sleep. Fat chance of that! Every other night (my night 'on' in the shift system my husband and I share) I go through the same struggle inside of my head. Do I let him play and then feel like I'm a really useless parent? Or, do I switch the light off, haul him into bed and spend the next two hours in an experience that can only be described as wrestling with a tiger? Whatever I do there's normally a point I'll reach of total exhaustion, despair and helplessness all mixed in together, where I wonder 'How the hell did we end up with a life like this?'

The family

There can be so much focus on the child with disabilities that we forget the effect it can have on our other children and our partners. Difficult behaviour can put a strain on all the relationships within the family and on family life itself. There are many examples of this but a few that come to mind are:

- The child with special needs screaming and making a scene in public causing embarrassment to brothers and sisters as well as parents.

- Exhausted parents who, after countless sleepless nights, have no energy for each other or their other children.

- The child with special needs is often pacified and their demands are always allowed for fear of the tantrum that will occur if this is not the case.

📖 Parent's story

Every evening our house is a battleground. Ryan gets aggressive with his brothers and is very violent, but luckily the other two understand.

Often, family life can become really strange; everything is reversed. We get used to living abnormal lives, and our other children have to too.

Moving on

Ways of being

When considering what we can do to tackle the behaviour a lot of books talk about behaviour strategies, techniques and management. As a parent my major concern is to keep sane and have a healthy home life. I don't think there is one answer. Every family and every child are different; there are many and varied ways of doing things. However, I do think that change is possible and whatever you do starts inside you. Most children at one time or another misbehave. With children with special needs the chances of this happening are greater as they have many more difficulties managing to live in our world. So, if this is our reality what we need is to clear our heads and have time to think so we can work out what to do. We need to be able to think clearly and be resourceful and creative. For most of us, getting to that point requires spending some time considering how we feel and some of the belief systems we've built up about ourselves.

Daring to hope

When things are getting out of hand one of the bravest things any parent with a child with a disability can do is to hope that things will change. That can seem a dangerous thing to think, but actually not hoping is more dangerous as it means believing that things will stay exactly like this or get worse. And yet it's easier to stay believing the worst. It's quite a safe place; it doesn't challenge anything.

Admitting to difficult emotions

The other brave thing to do is to admit to how we really feel. That's a fairly tall order. In Chapter 2, we looked at finding a 'listener': someone who is accepting and non-judgemental who can hear how we feel without giving us advice. Listeners can really help us admit to difficult emotions; it's often hard to do it on our own. Talking about feelings helps us get beyond guilt. Guilt paralyses you and freezes you up. You can spend a lot of time regretting the past. The phrase, 'if only' comes to mind. 'If only I hadn't smoked when I was pregnant maybe he wouldn't have been born with all these problems.' It's inevitable that we will do this but if we spend all our time thinking of the past, it leaves no time for the problems of today. Guilt can also cause you to be indecisive; afraid of doing anything for fear of making it worse. Also it can cause you to spend a lot of your life compensating for the fact that your child has a disability.

 **Parent's story**

I'm always asking myself: 'Where did I go wrong? What if I didn't do enough?'

The fact is that children with special needs often put enormous pressure on parents. We are human beings and human beings put under that sort of pressure feel unexpected things. The hard issue to deal with is that we have unexpected feelings about our own children. Feelings such as:

- Fear

  We can feel as if we're out of control because our child's actions are unpredictable and we can't understand them.

- Deep hurt

  We try really hard and do all the normal things that parents do and we get the opposite reaction to what we were expecting.

- Anger

  Our anger can be really extreme. We can feel very violent and sometimes we might wish they were dead.

- Disappointment

  Somewhere deep down, there is often a lot of disappointment; you want normal things from your child that other people get, like politeness, 'A's in maths and a football medal for playing in the school team.

- Embarrassment

  When our children do strange things in public, people look and judge us as parents.

- Shame

  Shame is a deeper feeling than guilt. It's what we often feel when our child does something really unacceptable in society's terms like smearing faeces all over the living room walls. It's also what we feel when in an intense moment we've just wished they weren't in our lives.

📖 Parent's story

If I started hitting I wouldn't stop.

📖 Parent's story

You get used to disappointment. I helped Brandon practise for his concert at Easter, and then he laid on the floor for two-thirds of it, the only child in nursery who did. I was really looking forward to that concert; I went home afterwards and cried.

📖 Parent's story

When Tayo sat on everyone's lap at the GPs, I felt so embarrassed.

☞ My story

One time, I found myself imagining what life would be like if Jonathan wasn't alive. What I'd being doing, the places we'd go. When I came to, I was horrified; I'd just wished my son dead and I felt so ashamed.

Clearing our head and looking at our belief systems

Expressing difficult emotions is almost always a relief and it means that we now have space to work out what is going on.

The first thing to look at is the belief systems that have built up that are often behind these difficult emotions.

Belief 1

'I'm a useless parent and there is nothing I can do that will change anything.'

This is a common belief that I certainly had. The ridiculous thing is that most of us are doing an exceptional job under very trying circumstances. One way of thinking about this is to imagine anyone who makes critical comments to you, be that a teacher, an occupational therapist or a friend, coming and living in your house for 24 hours and seeing how they cope.

The truth is the opposite; we as parents are in fact the child's best chance. Our knowledge, our love, our lifetime interest are far more powerful and will provide far more resources than any therapy or professional will ever provide. Believing it is for some of us is a long journey, but a good place to start is giving yourself a positive message rather than all the negative ones you've been listening to. Saying to yourself something like: 'I am a good parent, I do love my child and I can make a difference.'

Belief 2

'I daren't change anything at home, if I do all hell will break loose.'

Change itself is often too frightening to think about. We as parents can get into a cycle with some children where it seems no matter what is tried, nothing changes. There seems to be no co-operation from the child at all just a lot of chaos and destruction. So you settle for a system for the sake of peace where most of what the child demands is allowed because without it tantrums follow. The scene below is not a parent's story but could easily happen.

> Fatima wants to play on the computer all day, laughing at the screen, obeying the commands. She's very good with the computer for three years old. But, her mum has to collect her sister from the playgroup and this gets in the way of Fatima's playing time. She's played on the computer for three hours but to get her away, she has to be physically manhandled and dragged away while her mother has chunks of her hair pulled out. Sometimes, Fatima's mother gives up and her sister doesn't go to playgroup because she can't face it.

In such a situation the payback for the parent is terrible. It causes all sorts of feelings but especially despair and helplessness. When

Parent's story

From an early age with Amy, I've had negative feelings from other people. I started to believe it was my fault.

Parent's story

I've started to realise that I am the expert where Samuel is concerned, no one else.

Parent's story

I have no life of my own, I just have to follow his routines.

I went through this stage what I noticed is how switched off I became, not just as a parent but also as a person.

> ☞   **My story**
>
> When Jonathan was four and we were at the height of awful nights and difficult days I think our family shut down for a while. We existed on day-to-day crisis management. We didn't go out or do anything. We just survived. I think at that point if people asked me if anything was going to change I would have felt very defensive. Quite honestly the thought terrified me. It was enough just to get through the day; the thought of doing things any differently was too much.

Belief 3

'The problem is this child's behaviour. I'm going to punish him so badly, he won't know what's hit him.'

If you have been brought up to believe that children should behave well for their parents then the way your child is behaving is way off your scale of values. So a common response is to punish them, to try and control their behaviour. Here are a few thoughts on why punishment is not a good solution.

1 It's not practical – When we punish the child with special needs she often responds with even worse behaviour. We might physically force them to do something and often violence is involved. From this point on, whatever the outcome, both child and parent lose. Sometimes the cycle continues with things getting really out of hand and quite extreme. But crucially, often the parent is left feeling powerless as well as angry and the child feels angry too and is not encouraged to change her behaviour.

2 The child doesn't learn anything – The word discipline comes from the word disciple which is a learner; most of the time children learn very little about behaviour through being punished. Evidence suggests that punishment does not teach a child to stop misbehaving it just pushes the behaviour somewhere else (Donnellan *et al.* 1988). What does work though is consistent, logical and, if possible, natural consequences and boundaries.

3 It's not fair – In *Understanding ADHD* Christopher Green and Kit Chee (1997) make the point that if a child is physically impaired so that he is wheelchair bound you wouldn't force him to run and if a child is deaf you wouldn't shout at them until they

could hear. And yet, parents are often prepared to push and punish children for their behaviour that is actually part of their condition.

4 It robs the parent of a loving relationship with their child – The previous chapter on communication talked of the loving relationship between parent and child being central to everything. If you make a child obey through fear you might succeed, but what you lose is their love and respect.

Belief 4

'*This child is deliberately trying to hurt me.*'
There are times when children are deliberate in their actions towards you, but there are very many times when children with special needs are just trying to look after themselves the best way they know. The action is not deliberately aimed at you. However, when it comes out of nowhere, it can feel as though it is directed at you and then it can really hurt emotionally.

> ### ☞   My story
>
> I can think of some examples of this with my own children. A few weeks ago, the school minibus that picks Jonathan up for school was very late. Jonathan understood this because Carys had left for school and he was still waiting. Children on the autistic spectrum learn to put their trust in routines that happen every day. So when the minibus still didn't arrive, Jonathan became very agitated and started to pinch and scratch me.
>
>   A much milder version of this happens with Carys. Sometimes when I pick her up from school, I get a barrage of shouting. I've learnt that this is not for me; it's a build up of frustration at having to cope all day at school. A lot of parents whose children have specific learning difficulties or ADHD report the same thing.

Belief 5

'*This child is ruining my life; my life is a total nightmare.*'
A response such as this often comes from very tired, desperate parents who are at the end of their tether. If people were really honest, many parents with children, whether they have special needs or not, have at some point felt like this. I have certainly had my share of 4 a.m. spots feeling like that. If, however it becomes a persistent feeling that becomes hard to dislodge it can become a self-fulfilling prophecy: parents' lives do become ruined. It's incredibly important to find out where such a belief comes from. It's often a lot of stored up grief and loss that needs to be expressed.

It's also really important to rethink your view of your child. Children are complicated, capable of wonderful and terrible things all in the same hour. When we feel our child is ruining our lives we've lost our sense of their positive qualities. This is often not helped by our experience with diagnosis or education. By the time a child is five, she may have already picked up a lot of labels attached to her behaviour and condition, such as autistic, developmentally delayed, brain impaired, ADHD or challenging behaviour. Often these labels will make parents feel like something 'bad' has happened to their child and to them. Take for example, when you go to parents' evening and hear some unexpected news from a teacher.

> When Anne, Rosie's mum went to parents' evening, she was told:
>
> 'There's something wrong, Rosie is very backward, she can't understand and she doesn't know how to talk to the other children.'
>
> Anne was really shocked and suddenly in her mind's eye Rosie changed and became a problem; she became an embarrassment and a disappointment. It was only when Anne spoke to a friend who reminded her, 'She's still Rosie, she hasn't turned into a monster,' that she was able to let go of these feelings.

Sometimes these feelings that your child is damaged and lacking in some way can be harder to shift. However, I think it's really important that we challenge these feelings and hold on to what we like about our children. We live in a society where the way we use words to describe ourselves defines who we are. It may seem incredibly hard to remember positive things when every day you face daily power struggles, defiance and temper tantrums. Yet, the importance of holding on to the positive qualities of your child cannot be understated.

To respond to a child's behaviour in a helpful way that is really going to make a difference at least some part of you has to like them.

☞ My story

> When Jonathan was diagnosed and we got all these medical reports it gave you no sense of who he was. I wanted to shout 'But he's a good cuddler and he's a lot of fun and he loves trains.'

Ideas and strategies

Looking at your belief systems and attitudes has to be the first step to tackling behaviour. The next step is considering some strategies and ideas that might work at home for you.

General ideas – a behaviour toolkit

Children are unique and so are their parents. It seems to me that the best way of looking at behaviour is to have a variety of ideas available to use when appropriate. I developed this idea through observing my husband when he does DIY (we're very stereotyped in our family in that department). He has a large red metal toolbox and for each job he might take out three or four tools but it won't necessarily be the same tools; each job is different. It's the same with our children; the way we deal with their behaviour is individual to each child, depending just as much on personality as it does on disability. The ideas and strategies that follow can be used as a springboard to develop your own behaviour toolkit that works for you and your child.

Looking after yourself

I make no apology for making looking after yourself the first tool at your disposal. The fact is unless you build up your resources, it will be very difficult to consider any other of the ideas that follow. Dealing with children's behaviour is the hardest part of any parent's job, but for a parent of a child with special needs it can be incredibly tough. Looking after our own needs is often very low down our list of priorities, but because many of us face very difficult situations we need to take into account our own needs. Looking after ourselves does not have to involve big things, in fact if you think big you're less likely to do it. It's much more realistic to plan small regular activities that are for you, such as:

- getting a babysitter and going out with your partner
- reading a good book
- doing some sport
- seeing a friend for a drink
- sitting down at home with the children and deciding that, unless it is a matter of life or death, you are not going to move from this chair and this cup of tea for a least 20 minutes.

Listening

Start to think of behaviour as a way of communication (in the last chapter we touched on this). For some children without speech their only option is to behave in such a way that they are noticed and their needs are met. As Michael W. Small in 'Revisiting choice' comments: 'A number of people with disabilities have learned to "shout" with their behaviour because it is the only way that they are heard' (O'Brien and O'Brien 1998: 39). Those children with speech still have major problems communicating what they want; getting your attention through behaviour is often much easier for them. Listening well is a bit like being a detective. Follow the trail of this behaviour, where did it start, what was the trigger?

Stepping back

When you're the parent of a child with special needs, it's very hard to step back. There are many reasons for this. We are naturally afraid for them; there is often a strong desire to overprotect them and hold them back from danger. Also we are worried about what they might do; their behaviour can be unpredictable to say the least. Sometimes they may be aggressive and some of our children have no sense of danger. Many of us, me included, remain in a state of hyper-vigilance, permanently anxious about what might happen next. And yet I'm aware from my own experience that my anxiety can actually hold my children back. They can feel restricted and they are not able to grow and develop. So, as parents we face a huge dilemma: whether to step back a bit and see what happens or step in to protect our child and in some cases other children. I've been helped in my thinking on this by a little article I found while researching the book. It was written in 1984 in America by the parent of an autistic child, Mary S. Ackerley. She offers some really down to earth points about this problem:

■ Our children are still children first and their disability comes second, so if you're thinking through a particular situation with your child, ask yourself: If he didn't have special needs what would the answer be? Why does it have to be different for him? Sometimes there are good reasons why it has to be different but sometimes the only thing that's stopping him doing something is your anxiety.

■ It is not so terrible to make an honest wrong decision. This is great advice; we have this sense with our children that we have to be perfect in all we do with them and if something goes wrong, it's absolutely terrible. It's not.

■ All parents at some stage make mistakes with all their children. Mistakes are nothing to feel guilty about, they are a normal part of every family's process. Often the best way you learn and develop an idea is through something not working out in the way you planned.

Stepping back has led me to think and react differently – it is a new perspective and approach. I'm still aware that my children need protecting from the world but I'm becoming more aware that sometimes my anxiety can box them in. For them to grow and develop into the unique individuals that they are, they need me to let go a bit and take some risks.

Understanding behaviour

We stand a much greater chance of working out what to do with our child's behaviour if we try and understand why a child is behaving the way they are. I think that gets us at least 75 per cent of the way to doing something about it.

All children, whether they have disabilities or not, want to feel good about themselves and want to feel important and connected to their parents. If this isn't happening for them there is a strong possibility that they'll show it through their behaviour. Difficult behaviour may result because the child:

- wants attention – 'I want you to notice me and care about me.' The child could be: hungry, sleepy, scared, over stimulated, bored or under stimulated, frustrated, having an allergic reaction or feeling ill. Things are made worse when we try to stop the behaviour without finding out what the child wants. The behaviour may be the only way the child can express his needs or wants.

- wants power – 'I can do what I want, where I want, when I want to.' From time to time every child wants to take control of his surroundings – it's the first step to independence. Temper tantrums are the best example of this.

- is showing helplessness – 'Nothing I do makes any difference to you! Well forget it! I'm not doing anything.' The child is feeling very discouraged.

- wants revenge – 'So you don't think I don't matter much, do you? Well I'll show you a thing or two!' When children hurt they can show difficult behaviour to 'get even'.

Types of behaviour

As well as understanding the reasons that may prompt difficult behaviour, it's also useful to consider the types of behaviour that children with special needs can show. These can include:

- Challenging behaviour

  The key here is that our families have to cope on an everyday level with behaviour that other families might experience occasionally, for example noise, strange mannerisms, aggression, destruction and self-harming behaviour to name but a few. Challenging behaviour is not just this type of behaviour though, it's how extreme it is and the amount of times it happens.

- Behaviour associated with learning difficulties

  This is best described as lots of gaps, that is behaviour you would expect of a much younger child. Independence skills, such as dressing and undressing, toileting and eating without help, are slow in developing.

- Behaviour associated with a speech and language disorder

  There is often difficulty with language in terms of understanding or speaking.

Your child's condition

Generally a child with special needs behaviour will be affected by their condition. In fact, their behaviour can often reflect the way they have made sense and compensated for the world in which they live. Therefore the more you learn about your child's condition the easier it will be to answer the question: 'How is this impairment affecting his behaviour?' There are good books and websites to visit that give you a picture of what is going on (see the Resource directory for more details).

☞ My story

Take Jonathan for example:

- He seems obstinate and rude when actually he does not understand.

- He seems selfish and uncaring when actually he has no idea of the effect he is having on other people's emotions.

- His violent behaviour makes him frightening and unpredictable when actually he is scared stiff of the people around him.

- He is naughty all the time and does not respond to punishment, when actually he finds it hard to learn from his mistakes because he doesn't remember them.

- He can be weird and bizarre and uncomfortable to be around when he gets into one of his obsessive behaviours. Such behaviour includes: lying face down on a manhole cover and licking it; rewinding, fast-forwarding and ejecting videos for hours; and dragging all the bedding and cushions from the house and piling it up in one big pile. When actually he is just trying to meet his own needs in the best way he can.

Trigger points

There are certain situations that can trigger difficult behaviour in children, or make things a lot worse. If we've worked out what these are in advance, it will put us in a better position when something happens. It will be different for every child. This is about knowing how your child ticks – the question you need to ask is: what sort of events, occasions and circumstances generally prove difficult for your child? It may be one or more of the following:

- Place – The size of the room, be that living room, bedroom or classroom at school, can be important. Some children with special needs may have a sense of their personal space being invaded if you come within a few metres of them. The room the child is mainly in at school or home might have changed. There might be changes to the décor of the room; certain colours can be disturbing and might set off a reaction, other colours might be calming. Furniture or objects in the room might be moved; we may regard them as rubbish but to the child they are well loved and valuable.

- Sound – For some children the overall level of noise can be a distraction. For others, particularly those on the autistic spectrum, certain sounds can be painful.

- People – New people, be that visitors at home or new teachers at school, can cause confusion. They may not be as predictable or as consistent as before and if they are confrontational, heaven help you! It may be worth considering whether there are people around your child doing something to provoke the child. They may not be aware they're doing it.

- Changes in routine – A seemingly small change to us can make a huge difference children with special needs. Sometimes, as parents we might miss little changes.

- Illness – Your child can be ill and not able to tell you.

- Diet – Has their diet changed in any way? Has new food been introduced that might have caused a reaction?

- External stress – My theory is that children, particularly children with disabilities, can be like the 'emotional thermometer' in a family. Children with disabilities are far more likely to express the results of financial problems, divorce, remarriage, step siblings, living with single parents, drugs, domestic violence, unemployment, relationships problems between couples and bereavement through behaviour than any other member of a family. The results in children can be restlessness, difficulty concentrating, irritating behaviour, depression or severe anxiety. It's worth noting that even events that are good, exciting and parents might see as positive can be stressful for children with special needs. Such examples might include: mother starting a college course, father getting a promotion at work, parties and holidays. Also children have a habit of reacting 'after the event', so it's sometimes hard to work out that the family stress is the trigger.

Have a home atmosphere of nurture

Any child gets on best in an atmosphere of peace, calmness, gentleness and encouragement. This is particularly true of children with special needs who cope really badly around conflict, faultfinding and negativity. Christopher Green and Kit Chee in *Understanding ADHD* say: 'Nice kids remain nice when accepted as they are, given realistic limits, guided, rewarded, enjoyed and loved. They don't want to be managed by force or fear, they need a parent who is a supporter, a believer and a friend' (Green and Chee 1997: 58).

Be enthusiastic and excited when they do what we want

Often as parents, our big reactions go to the difficult behaviour and our small boring reactions go to the times when the child is doing really well. Or, they get no reaction at all and we go off and do the washing up! Yet imagine the scene if we didn't take anything for granted, where every effort at good behaviour, any attempt at communication, and any small move to independence was celebrated and commented on. It's worth thinking what message that would give to your child. It says:

- I am so proud of the effort you are putting in here.
- I've noticed how hard you're working.
- I am really interested in you.

It builds up self-esteem and confidence and encourages children to keep going.

Be patient

You need to remember you're in for the long haul. Look for small steady changes rather than overnight transformation. Keeping your expectations realistic but hopeful is the best option.

Survival

For the sake of sanity, learn flexibility and an acceptance of present reality. For example, you are asking for a nervous breakdown if you get upset every time food gets dropped on the floor when your child's latest game is really climbing on roofs. It's important to decide which battles are worth fighting. Having done that, it's easier to accept some things, such as the fact your house isn't going to be the tidiest in the world and your child's eating habits aren't the best. Doing so gives you more energy for other things.

Anticipation

Most parents can see trouble coming: the explosions tend to have warnings attached. If you can get in there before the explosion and divert and distract you can save yourself a lot of time and energy.

Have a home where it's OK to have emotions

'There is a difference between being angry and hitting your brother.' It's really important for children (and adults) that their emotions are listened to and recognised as important. Parents can show this in the way they treat each other as well as their children. Sometimes we all need to be noticed.

Be aware of cycles of behaviour

Cycles of behaviour are when difficult behaviour by one family member triggers reactions by other members of the family. This happens at some stage in most families. It has to do with the amount of stress the family is under, which is why it often happens at teatime when the children are hungry and tired and parents are rushing around trying to do a number of tasks at once. However, it's more likely to happen in a family with a child with a disability because we are under more stress (for more details on stress see the next chapter) and children with some special needs are more likely to do things that trigger a large family reaction. For example, picture the scene:

Waqis is an eight-year-old boy with Asperger's syndrome and ADHD. His little brother Abdul, who is five, won't leave him alone. Abdul is teasing him and keeps taking his cars away. Abdul is making a lot of noise. Waqis gets really frustrated and bites Abdul, who immediately starts screaming. His mother Nazneen runs in from the kitchen to see what's going on. Abdul continues screaming but shows her bite marks. Nazneen shouts at Waqis who starts crying, at which point his father Omar walks in and hearing Nazneen shout at Waqis tells her off. Nazneen is really angry with Omar so shouts back at him.

So as one parent I interviewed put it: 'Before you know where you are, the house is in uproar.' Sometimes it can't be avoided but a way to calm things down is to think about our reactions as parents; the way we speak to each other and our children could make all the difference.

Routines and rituals

I think routines and family rituals are a really important stress buster. Children with special needs find them really helpful and generally, families know where they are; we're all happier when life is predictable and we know where we stand. Even when chaos rears its ugly head in the form of illness or no sleep, rituals and routines can save the day. It can be such ideas as developing a bedtime routine or simple little rituals that you and your family always do.

Rewards

There are some dangers with using rewards, particularly complicated reward systems that can take over a parent's life. However, to be rewarded and appreciated for something we've done is something all human beings enjoy. The keys are:

- Rewards should never replace praise, encouragement and enthusiasm for good behaviour.

- Rewards are not bribes, for example 'If you do this, I'll . . .', otherwise the only motivation for good behaviour is what they're going to get.

- Keep rewards simple and immediate. With children with autism for example, the reward is called a reinforcer and is given directly after good behaviour happens.

- Focus by choosing one area of behaviour to work on at a time so the child is clear what she is being rewarded for.

- Make sure the reward is something the child actually wants.

- Rewards don't have to be material: back rubs, singing, blowing bubbles, special time with Mum all work well.

Be consistent and clear

Have a few fair consistent rules that are easily understood. All children need boundaries but children with special needs who have so many difficulties understanding our world need a safe protected place at home; boundaries help them to feel safe. Two important points:

- Have just a few boundaries or rules. If you have lots of rules with a child with special needs, especially one with little understanding of how to behave socially, you'll end up being an enforcer rather than a parent.

■ Be consistent. This is hard because we're only human, but children with special needs understand things better if boundaries stay the same rather than change. It's much easier to be consistent if you have only a few boundaries.

Rules and consequence

There's no point having boundaries unless when they are challenged you respond. But it's how you respond that is all-important. This is the moment that can make things a lot better and a whole lot worse. The key points are:

■ Beware of big angry scenes – We're all human and when faced with devastation to our living room, it's not surprising that we explode. But practically, explosion simply adds fuel to the fire for two important reasons:

1 It's more than likely to escalate the situation; a lot of verbal children with special needs will at this point lock horns with you. It then becomes a battle and in this battle the casualty will always be damage to your relationship with your child.

2 When you explode you are entertaining to your child – many children with special needs, particularly those who have difficulties processing social information, really enjoy your reaction. In fact they'll repeat their difficult behaviour just to see you do it again.

☞ **My story**

When we shout at Jonathan after he's run away he sees a red face, angry eyes and he hears an angry tone of voice and to him it's interesting and exciting. He doesn't connect with the fact that we're angry but he might do it again just to get the same reaction.

■ When you're thinking of consequences, if they are long and drawn out they are unlikely to work. They don't make very much sense to the child, so they forget why it's happening. Also, it takes so much energy for you to keep it up, that it can end up being more of a punishment for you. It is better to have natural and simple consequences that are related to what just happened. For example, it makes more sense to children if when they break a toy they don't get another one, rather than 'You won't have any pocket money next week.'

- Be firm without the fireworks – If it's a dangerous situation it may need a quick physical reaction, like pulling the child off the road, but not a big emotional outburst.

- Focus on being calm. This takes a bit of work and is back to belief systems. Ask yourself what you are afraid of here.

- Your face needs to show very little emotion.

- Talk in a soft calm voice and use simple language that doesn't condemn the child: 'It's OK now, let's sit down.'

- Avoid eye contact, approaching too fast, leaning forward, raising your voice, making threats, giving orders and using fast, quick body movements.

- Be matter of fact: 'This is the way it is.' If the child is verbal keep away from long complicated explanations or arguments.

Using time out

This does not mean long periods of time in a locked room with no privileges. Time out works best as a brief cooling off space for parent and child – we often need it as much as them! It gives the child a place to calm down and begin to solve her own problems. It might be the place to go to dance or jump on their trampoline (let off some physical energy) or talk themselves down, write or draw (using creative energy). Time out does not have to be a bedroom, it might be the garden or a walk and can be explained to the child as 'calm down time'.

Use relaxation techniques

Children with special needs often respond really well to relaxation techniques that help them to calm down, such as deep breathing and massage. These techniques don't just help to calm and relax children they have many other positive benefits. On a simple level it's a way of having fun with your child in a very special one-to-one way. It can decrease aggression and increase self-esteem and concentration. If your relationship is going through a sticky patch it can restore that feeling of enjoying each other's company and it's good for you as well as them. Finally, and I say this from my own experience, it can help children sleep!

Look at the child's diet

Many parents in this country are choosing to look at their child's diet. For example, some are:

- choosing to opt for a gluten- and/or dairy-free diet (particularly for children with autism or ADHD). There is now a growing body of research pointing to the benefits of doing this (for details see the Austim Research Unit under 'Therapies and treatments' in the Resource directory).

■ keeping food diaries, noting certain foods that seem to trigger a child's behaviour and then removing them from the diet. Common offenders include chocolate, coke, strawberries and artificial sweeteners.

■ choosing to add vitamins and minerals to the diet. These include multi-vitamins but also evening primrose oil and fish oil. Again new research is suggesting that including these in your child's diet can improve co-ordination and the ability to process information (for details see Autism Research Unit in the Resource directory).

☞ My story

Two years ago, after receiving medical advice, we put Jonathan on a gluten- and dairy-free diet. Although it was hard work at first we've seen some real improvements: a decrease in hyperactivity and destructiveness and an increase in his abilities to concentrate and focus. Crucially for us though, two things happened: some time after we started the diet Jonathan seemed to emerge out of his own little world and come and join ours for periods of time, opening up the possibility of communication; and, over a longer period of time, his sleep improved.

If you're thinking about changing your child's diet:

■ Do it properly under the supervision of a doctor or dietician.

■ Plan it like a military operation; it's not something you can just do overnight, you need to research and get alternative foods.

■ Read up on it. There are lots of good websites and books (see Resource directory).

■ Tell everyone who looks after your child what you are doing and why.

■ Keep a food diary before and after you make any changes.

■ Be patient; it sometimes takes up to six months to see the real benefits.

Reduce the background sensory information at home

Some children with special needs become very distressed in the presence of certain sounds, sights and touch. The inputs are those that others would take for granted and would process easily.

☞ My story

It was only after I'd been at a conference on autism that I realised how much sensory information I expect my children to process at once. Consider the sensory information in the kitchen:

- Foods cooking (smell);
- I want them to eat their tea (taste);
- The radio, washing machine and dishwasher are on all at the same time (sound);
- I'm wearing my bright red jumper, which Jonathan always tries to remove from me (sight);
- I'm talking and asking them questions (sound).

I've discovered that if I turn the radio, dishwasher and washing machine off and leave my red jumper in the wardrobe, Jonathan stays at the table and gives me eye contact and Carys is calmer and better behaved.

Reduce the amount of TV, video or PlayStation they see

As we have just noted many children with special needs already have difficulties taking the normal everyday information from the world around them; watching too many videos and computer games overloads their systems. Further, if they have:

- hyperactive behaviour or they don't sleep very well it is likely to make matters worse.
- speech and language difficulties, watching TV or video does not encourage eye contact and all the things you need to have a conversation with someone.

I'm not saying get rid of TV, video and PlayStation. This book would not have been written without *Thomas the Tank Engine* videos. As parents things have to get done and this is an easy way of occupying children, but if you can reduce the time spent and find other more interesting things for them to do in the long run everyone benefits.

Specific ideas

The ideas in this section are specific to different disabilities, however, this is only ever meant to be a rough guide. Children have a habit of refusing to stay in the 'boxes' we put them in.

The following ideas have been shown to work well with children with severe or moderate learning difficulties and with children on the autistic spectrum who have severe or moderate difficulties. Sources of information for this section are Jordan (2001) and Clements and Zarkowska (2000).

Introducing alternative behaviours

Find an alternative behaviour that satisfies the same need as the unwanted behaviour in that it reduces stress, but it doesn't hurt the child or others, or is more socially acceptable. For example:

- something different to do with their hands rather than scratching; or

- using the toilet rather than the floor to wee on.

The alternative behaviour needs to be used a lot so it becomes a habit.

☞ My story

When Jonathan pinches, it's often his way of saying he is overexcited (professionals call it over-aroused). This is why he does it with a smile on his face! If we squeeze his hands or put some heavy pressure on his shoulders, while firmly saying 'No pinching', it helps calm him down and is actually more enjoyable to him than pinching.

Diversion

Divert to something else if you can. Diversion is a surprisingly good, simple tactic, particularly if you can distract the child before matters have got out of hand.

Breaking down a task

This is a way of encouraging children with disabilities to move from helplessness to independence. A parent once told me that breaking down the action of going to the toilet involved 14 different actions. For some children remembering the actions in the right order is really hard work. What they need from parents is understanding, patience, praise but also, crucially, the ability to hold back and wait, rather than jumping in and finishing off the action for the child. As parents we do this because we're frustrated but waiting 30 seconds isn't that long and it's only through waiting that we discover he actually can pull his own pants up!

Prompting

This is also a way of encouraging independence. It works in three stages:

1 Physical – Child's body is moved by the parent to do the action, for example turning a tap on. That way the child learns what the action feels like. Gradually as the child is able to turn the tap on himself the parent fades into the background.

2 Gesture – Show a child the action, for example if you want him to sit down, pat the seat.

3 Verbal – Say the action, 'Sit down' at first with the gesture as well and then gradually use the words on their own.

These ideas have been shown to work with children with mild learning difficulties, Asperger's syndrome, ADHD, specific learning difficulties and other communication disorders.

Teach self-talk skills

For most people, 'inside talking' and doing things are linked; we learn to talk ourselves down in stressful situations. We become skilled at processing stress and difficulty through talking it through in our heads. In this way we can calm ourselves down and decide what we're going to do. Some children do not find this easy and some emotions are more difficult to control and can end up being acted out in difficult behaviour. At the same time, thinking and planning ahead are abandoned. So we need to teach our children to talk to themselves! Self-talking can be used in a number of ways:

- as a means of controlling anger and developing self-control and reflection (e.g. Teach him to say one or two phrases to himself when someone provokes him, such as 'Keep cool', or 'Relax').

- helping children organise themselves and to remember problem-solving ideas (e.g. Teach her a phrase that will serve as a prompt to start a set of actions, such as 'Now let's see where do we begin?', which might be followed by 'OK that's done. What do I do next?').

- helping children have a more positive image of themselves (e.g. Most children use negative self-talk like 'I'm stupid', so it's turning this into positive self-talk, such as 'I can do it if I try.').

- helping children to be more assertive in stressful situations.

📖 **Parent's story**

I teach phrases like: 'I don't like it', 'Keep out of my space', and 'Leave me alone', to stop him hitting out.

Teach problem solving

Children with special needs often have many problems: conflict with their family, school difficulties and problems making and keeping friends. Their response to these problems is to act out feelings of anger, disappointment or rage through behaviour rather than thinking about why they feel so bad.

There are three things you want them to think about:

1 What is the problem? – Get children to describe their problem as precisely as possible.

2 How do you feel when it happens?

3 How can I solve it? – It's great when children discover that they can solve their own problems, that they have choices and options. It encourages them to be independent.

This is connected to the ideas about 'emotional intelligence', we looked at in Chapter 3.

Where problem solving is concerned, you also want to help them think through strategies for future problems, particularly issues at school where things can flare up really quickly. A friend, who is a home–school worker, says that at her school, children who have behavioural or concentration difficulties are encouraged to find a trusted adult and tell them if they are feeling upset or angry and ask to go out of class for 10 minutes. Apparently it works really well.

☞ My story

Carys is really good verbally but suffers from volcanic explosions of anger mostly directed at her parents, often due to problems at school. So we have been teaching her to connect feelings to action and then problem solve. The most helpful way for us has been to teach her the four-part message:

■ I feel

■ When

■ Because

■ What can I do about it?

This links feelings about events to problem solving. One day recently after a fairly loud exchange I found Carys in her room dancing. When I asked her why, she said: 'When I'm angry, dancing helps me calm down.' She'd worked out how she felt and problem solved a solution that worked.

Help your child to be resilient

Children with special needs have often been through a cycle of failure: experiencing repeated difficulty in class, low Standard Assessment Tests (SATs) results, feeling different to other people at school, finding it hard to keep friends and receiving criticism at home. The result is they give up; they feel a failure and they don't believe they can learn anything. Children begin to view things that happen to them as being beyond their control. If they do well, it's because of easy questions or a kind teacher. If they do badly, it's a mean teacher or because they're useless.

I think this is a real tough issue to deal with and for parents can be heartbreaking. Some ideas are:

■ No matter how small, notice and celebrate the successes and unless it's absolutely necessary don't comment on their weaknesses.

■ Comment on their bravery; it takes a lot of courage and determination to go back to school after a bad day or get back on that bike when you keep falling off.

■ Set your child up to succeed not to fail; encourage them to do things they are good at. Every child has some talent just waiting to be noticed. Be on the lookout for new activities where they might shine.

■ Spend time talking with him about the nature of his condition so as much as possible he understands why there may be difficulties.

Encourage children's creativity

Many children with special needs have huge reserves of creativity. They enjoy writing stories and poems, art, dance, drama and music. Encourage them at home by having things available, such as art materials, dressing-up clothes and music and then let them have a go without worrying too much about the mess! And outside the home look for supportive classes that might encourage their creativity. It's great for building confidence but it also helps them manage their emotions by giving them an outlet to express themselves.

Afterthought

Children's behaviour can be overwhelming at times; it can really drag you down. Sometimes it can be hard to make sense of anything. So if that's how you're feeling here are a few points that may help:

■ Don't try and deal with everything at once but look at which behaviour is causing you and your family the most stress.

- If that still doesn't narrow it down, Rita Jordan (2001) looked at the types of behaviours that it's worth considering first.

  Danger – When the behaviour is dangerous to him and others. This includes: hurting yourself, violence, running away and climbing in dangerous places.

  Effects on others – This behaviour goes beyond inconvenience, it really reduces the quality of people's lives around the child. Sleep disturbance is a good example of this.

  Restriction of life – This behaviour in itself is not bad, but when a child is so restricted, by for example refusing to go out, that their life and opportunities are taken away, then it may need looking at.

  Destruction – You measure this in terms of its severity and relentlessness. It's probably a good time to think about how to change things when you notice, for example, that furniture is continually being destroyed or tables at school are continually swept of objects.

  Socially unacceptable behaviour – To put it simply you want your child to survive in society. Any behaviour that is socially unacceptable needs looking at.

- Once you've decided what behaviour you want to deal with, have a plan. I have a very wise friend who when faced with her children's difficult behaviour spends time working out what she's going to do before she actually does anything. This is not always possible but it makes the difference between reacting to something and actually solving a problem or conflict.

- Don't go it alone, get everyone involved, school, friends and family and get their ideas and support. If there are some really stubborn difficulties, it's worth sitting down with your partner and some supportive friends and doing some brainstorming. If that doesn't seem possible at the moment, Chapter 8 'Hope' in this book looks at setting up a 'circle of support'.

- Don't be afraid to ask for help. It is not failure to ask for help, just a brave and honest realisation that the task is too big for one person.

- Accept the fact that there will be good days and bad days. A parent I interviewed put it so well, I leave the last comment to her.

📖 Parent's story

You can have days when you feel useless, you feel it's all your fault because you can't control his behaviour and other days when you think, 'He's not so bad after all'.

5 Stress

The way it is

> ### ☞ My story
>
> Today, my day started at 4 a.m. with Jonathan's happy screaming. By 6 a.m. I was up making homemade chicken nuggets (Jonathan is on a restricted diet and we'd run out of bread for his school lunch) while trying to persuade my son that a choc-ice wasn't the best idea for his breakfast. At 7.30 a.m. Carys woke up screaming because there was a fly in her bedroom. And by 9 a.m. I was at my desk at work with a mug of strong coffee writing a chapter on stress! There are many, many days when I, and parents like me, feel we live in alternative universes to other people. What we take to be 'normal' and take for granted, other people would view as a very high level of stress.

📖 Parent's story

Someone at school said: 'I couldn't get his coat on.' I thought: 'Couldn't get his coat on – you want to know what I've been through this morning . . .'

Being stressed is a very overused phrase. People can mean that they've had a bad experience at the hairdressers, or that they waited at home all day for a plumber and they didn't come. When parents of children with disabilities talk about stress it's completely different. We mean stretched so thinly that there doesn't seem to be anything left. We mean feeling so tired that we could sleep in any position, anywhere, for as long as we're allowed. Yet because we live in such high degrees of stress, we rarely have enough time to think of the reasons behind it. This chapter is an attempt to consider this. As usual it is split into two sections: 'The way it is' and 'Moving on'.

Real life stresses

📖 Parent's story

Home life is stressful, my life is lonely and I feel like I'm carrying a heavy load.

Everyday lives

The 'Positively Parents' study found that for most parents the stresses involved with bringing up a child with a disability were 'wide-ranging, unrelenting and sometimes overwhelming'

(Beresford 1994: 12). We can begin to get a picture of this, if we go through the normal parenting experience of parents of children with special needs. This includes:

- Meeting the child's physical or medical needs

  Not many parents have to learn advanced skills in nursing as part of ordinary day-to-day life; many of us do. To name just some of our skills: becoming experts in our child's medical condition, changing the nappies of squirming nine-year-olds and getting up several times a night to check oxygen tubes.

- Supervising or watching over the child

  Often we can be under a very intense type of stress where we have to keep an eye on our child all the time. A parent once described it as having eyes, not just in the back of her head, but also in her arms, legs and back. One of the stressful things is the unpredictability; everything may be fine for long periods of time and then for no apparent reason events spiral really quickly. This hyper-vigilance is very tiring and it makes it hard to switch off even when you can.

- Dealing with sleep and behaviour problems

  In the last chapter our focus was very much on what was going on for our child and how we could handle his behaviour. But how about the effect his behaviour has on us? The stress can be far reaching. Exhaustion can drain us of much of our energy and resources for life. It can also be wearing to live with the results of our child's behaviour – constant untidiness and random destruction.

- Seeing the child in pain or suffering from a life-threatening condition

  Jonathan has neither a life-threatening condition nor constant pain. Nevertheless my limited experience of the results of his bowel condition has been at times agony to watch. There is nothing more stressful than seeing your child doubled up in pain and being powerless to do anything. Parents who do live under the shadow of life-limiting conditions often live through daily trauma; the stress they are under is immense.

📖 Parent's story

You have to watch them constantly.

📖 Parent's story

I'm always on edge. Everything has to be planned out in advance; you always have to think ahead.

📖 Parent's story

I.have no sleep and I constantly feel like I'm shouting.

📖 Parent's story

I hate not having my home kept the way I would like.

Conflict with services

The 'Positively Parents' study found that 'Many parents had, at one time or another, been involved in some sort of confrontation with health, education or social services' (Beresford 1994: 39). This comment is backed up, not just by other reports nationally, but by my own experience and the network of parents I know. Conflict services is stressful and may arise for a variety of reasons.

Lack of services

One major source of stress is services that simply do not exist. Many parents have been through a carers' assessment with social services only to be told that, although we were entitled to everything, there were no services available and our only option was an extremely long waiting list. Parents in other parts of the country may fare better but in other ways, such as education and health, may have a worse experience.

Incompetence

Other sources of stress include incompetence in the way parents receive services. An example of this may be that your child is entitled to transport for school but it arrives at a different time each day. This may look like a small issue but for a child who understands through routine, it is a significantly distressing one.

Lack of understanding

The 'Positively Parents' study found that some professionals just did not have enough expertise; they frequently did not understand the needs of a child with a disability, particularly one with behavioural or learning difficulties (Beresford 1994: 35–49). Experiences like this mean that some of us feel let down and give up, thus being less likely to approach formal services in the future.

Education

The 'Positively Parents' study noted that the greatest source of stress for parents was conflict with services and this happened the most with the education department (Beresford 1994). Many parents find this extremely wearing.

Reactions of others

Negative reactions from others such as family or members of the public can be a great source of stress and distress for us. How many other parents, who don't have children with a disability, go through this experience?

Break up of parental relationship

Families who have a child with special needs can have severely limiting lives and this puts a big strain on everyone's mental health

---

📖 **Parent's story**

I get frustrated with his teacher and so does Joe. I feel because the disability can't be seen; she thinks there can't be one.

📖 **Parent's story**

You have to explain your child to strangers. You have to deal with other people's attitudes.

📖 **Parent's story**

My relatives don't understand; they are very ignorant about her condition. They say things like: 'You didn't give this girl proper training,' and 'You've spoiled her.' It makes me feel so bad.

and, particularly, on the parents' relationship. If there were cracks in the relationship before, bringing up a child with a disability will put more strain on the relationship. It's stressful when partners aren't getting on with each other and this is made worse by the fact that it's very difficult to find time alone to put something back into the relationship. The sad fact is that many couples do split up after having a child with special needs. In Chapter 7 'Families' we'll be considering in more detail ways of supporting relationships and ways of managing as a single parent.

Financial difficulties

In Chapter 2, 'Building up support', we looked at the fact that the parent who is the main carer of the child with a disability, rarely works. Apart from the difficulties of finding good childcare, there is also the likelihood that your child will have more illnesses, appointments and demands than other children. I know of one parent locally who was sacked because of the amount of time she had to have off work for her child. A recent change in the law is supposed to be giving working parents more flexibility, but has not been tested out yet. What this means is that most families with a child with a disability have only one wage earner and yet bringing up such a child is likely to be three times more expensive (Dobson and Middleton 1998). At times then, it is inevitable that for many of us it will be a financial struggle and, as we all know, money troubles are stressful.

The child

Parenting any child has no coffee breaks, sick leave or holidays attached, but parenting a child with special needs has an unrelenting quality about it. A friend of mine made a helpful observation about parenting Jonathan. She said: 'It's as if you have a toddler who never grows up.' There is a truth in that for children like Jonathan, his level of dependence and physical needs are like those of a toddler but he is six years old. Even with Carys, whose needs compared to Jonathan are mild, parenting is a full, time-consuming business. There is much to do in helping her process the world around her and manage it in a resilient way.

Parent's story

I envy other parents that can decide last minute trips and days out; everything with us has to be planned.

Expectations

Even before our children are born we have expectations about what they will be like and what our lives will be like as parents. Natural though they undoubtedly are, expectations lead to stress. In 1990 a study of families with Down's syndrome children from Scandinavian countries found that expectations had a direct effect on how parents felt about themselves (Kollberg *et al.* 1990). It discovered that expectations produced more stress in two key ways.

Expectation of freedom

Parent's story

I can't do a lot of things, which I normally enjoy doing again.

Normally, raising a child has future expectations. You expect to have a freer life as the child gets older and becomes more independent. You also expect to be able to develop as a person rather than just as a parent. This might mean work, social life or new hobbies. As the child grows older you see your friends developing their careers and moving into new interests yet you are just as tied as when your child was two. This can make you feel very stressed.

Expectations of being a parent

We live in a very goal-directed society. In schools, there are assessments, targets and tests. At work, there are goals, objectives and performance indicators. It becomes very easy to see being a parent that way. Parenting can become a project, where the object is to get your child through the hoops and progress onto the next stage. If you have that attitude to parenting and then have a child with special needs, it is possible to move from being a parent to someone who is another practitioner who gives your child treatment. If the child doesn't make progress with the therapy or the child appears to have different priorities to you this can become a major source of stress. Not only may it cause conflict with your child and cause you to question your parenting abilities but it also stops you from enjoying being with your child.

Feelings

Parent's story

The mental exhaustion is really bad. So much going on. You can't let your guard down, can't switch off because if you do something will happen. If one of my kids is quiet, I'm thinking what's going on?

According to the 'Positively Parents' study there was also 'considerable distress' for parents emotionally and mentally (Bresford 1994: 111). As well as these feelings of exhaustion, isolation and anger there are also some other feelings that definitely trigger stress – those of confusion and uncertainty. In a sense someone like Jonathan who has severe special needs is easier to deal with than a child with less of a disability because my expectations of him in terms of behaviour and general abilities are lower. However, for a child, such as Carys, who has a milder more hidden disability it is not clear what I as the parent can reasonably expect from her. This can and does lead to disagreements between Si and myself and with friends and family.

Parent's story

I'm more snappy, strained, tired and angry.

Health

All of this stress can impact on your health. Parents of children with disabilities experience many physical signs of stress, such as:

headaches, sleeplessness, breathlessness, high blood pressure, stomach troubles, back pain, lack of appetite and depression. These physical signs are often ignored, such is the pressure we are under. And yet these signs are a message from our bodies saying 'take five and look after yourself'.

Post-traumatic stress disorder

As I researched this chapter, it became clear to me that the daily stress for most parents with children with disabilities is incredibly high, and yet no one seems to notice. Parents who have children with special needs are rarely discussed on talk shows or are the subject of phone-ins. The nearest we get to being noticed is people saying, 'I don't know how you do it,' (to which I always want to reply, 'I don't have a choice'). As I said in the Introduction, we seem invisible in our society. Yet often we don't notice the stress ourselves. We get so used to this strange way of life, that we take it for granted.

> **📖 Parent's story**
>
> You're not living, just coping.

> **☞ My story**
>
> At Exchange, a few weeks ago, I asked one of the members of the group how her week had gone. She said, 'Oh just normal, nothing special,' I laughed in reply, 'You mean your normal evening where Tayo doesn't settle till 12 and you have to stay with him the whole time so you never get any time to yourself and then he wakes up at 5?' She smiled ruefully.

As time goes on we forget that most of the time we are living lives that are fairly close to the edge because we get used to the stresses of bringing up a child with special needs. Often we only really notice when there are other pressures like a death in the family, debt, unemployment and even the pressure of bringing up the rest of the family. Then we realise how vulnerable our families and we ourselves are. Barry and Sue Carpenter, parents of a child with special needs wrote: 'Chronic vulnerability is a constant state; it is part of being the parent of a child with special needs' (Carpenter and Carpenter 1997: 12). The Carpenters touch on something really important; I think many of us are living with the effects of post-traumatic and often present-traumatic stress disorder. And yet those around us do not acknowledge it and we seem unaware of it.

When I was researching this chapter I came across a definition by Garland (1991) for post-traumatic stress disorder: '*Experience of an event outside the range of usual human experience, which would be very distressing to anyone.*' I think that sums up pretty neatly what our lives can be like. If we swapped our lives with people we know, most of them would find it as difficult, stressful and distressing as we often do. And yet this definition is actually for people who have survived a disaster, big events like earthquakes or wars, something traumatic that happened in the past. And yet for us it's not just traumatic stress that happened in the past, it's extraordinary stress in the present that is likely to continue into the future.

'The symptoms'

The symptoms of post-traumatic stress disorder are in three main areas: feelings, actions and physical reactions (Pearlman date, Pearlman and Staub date). When I considered them closely they appeared to be very similar to many of the daily experiences I have in my own life and that of the people I knew with children with disabilities.

Feelings

There is a range of feelings linked to post-traumatic stress disorder, some of which have already been mentioned:

■ There is emotional numbness, blankness, not feeling anything. Earlier I commented on it as the times I have been in a robotic state; functioning but not feeling.

■ There is that feeling of not being able to cope with everyday situations I would normally expect to be able to manage, such as putting on Jono's shoes. This is something I feel all the time and it's often accompanied by a crushing sense of failure.

■ There is this enormous sense of guilt. This is often so strong for parents in our position that some of us find it hard to feel anything else. All the time, we're asking the question: 'What did I do wrong?'

■ There are the tears. I was never a person to cry regularly, yet in these past few years I often find myself crying at the slightest thing.

■ Finally, there are some assorted feelings that seem to come at me out of nowhere and can loosely be described as 'mood swings': irritability, anger, suspicion and fear.

Actions

These are some of the things that people who have post-traumatic stress disorder do:

- There is the tendency to isolate yourself from family and friends and social situations. Despite the fact that I know how important it is to be with others, when things are difficult at home my first instinct is stay there, cancel everything and hide. I'm not the only one who feels like this.

- There is a need for alcohol, drugs or 'comfort food' to get us through the day. Many parents, myself included, comfort eat and for me, alcohol consumption definitely goes up at times of high stress.

- It seems to be harder to make decisions or remember things. I always was a forgetful person but now, when things are really difficult at home, as well as losing my keys, purse and bag, I can forget people's names, where I am and what I was just doing. Although it sounds funny, sometimes it can be quite scary.

Physical reactions

These are some of the physical symptoms of post-traumatic stress disorder:

- Problems with sleeping – It seems bizarre that any of us should have trouble sleeping being that most of us are so tired. However, when times are really demanding at home, even when I have the chance, I don't sleep well, often suffering from disturbances and being unable to sleep for long periods.

- Easily startled; likely to jump when you hear a loud noise, having trouble concentrating and easily distracted – This is what I call feeling 'shaky'; like your nerve endings are jangling. I notice feeling like this in two separate circumstances: when something very traumatic has just happened, like one of Jono's near death experiences when he escapes out of the front door and runs into the middle of the road; or when a number of smaller things have happened one after another, like a screaming episode with Carys, followed by Jono flooding the bathroom, followed by the curtains being ripped down.

Parent's story

There was a stage a while back when I couldn't get out the front door. I was bottling everything up and I was really isolated.

Moving on

Ideas and strategies

I think there is real evidence to suggest that many parents of children with disabilities are experiencing such chronic stress on a day-by-day level that they actually have symptoms remarkably similar to post-traumatic stress disorder. This section is intended to be helpful to parents who feel they may be in this situation.

Priorities

It's really important to know what your priorities are in these circumstances. There are I think two crucial priorities: looking after yourself and asking for help.

Looking after yourself

I cannot emphasise how important it is to see looking after yourself as a priority. I know I may be repeating myself here, but it's not possible to give your child the care they need unless you start to think about *your* needs. Many parents look at me completely baffled when I say this. Given their lives they say how can they begin to think about looking after themselves. Consider the following points:

- Looking after you is a state of mind. It's about saying to yourself: 'I am important, I am valuable, I deserve some time off just like any other parent.' It's about giving yourself some credit next time things are really tough, for coping in incredibly difficult circumstances, instead of blaming yourself and feeling guilty for not coping.

- It's about grabbing time when it becomes available. When you're in the middle of a crisis, there is usually very little time, but sometimes unexpectedly you have a couple of hours to yourself – take it and don't feel guilty. 'But, but' I hear you cry 'the ironing, the washing, the cupboard under the stairs needs painting, that shelf needs fixing . . .'. They are not as important as *you*.

- Be creative – Sometimes it seems impossible to find time for yourself, but with a bit of creativity it's amazing what you can come up with. It's starting to see it as a problem that needs solving rather than an absolute impossibility.

> ☞ **My story**
>
> Si and I were finding it really hard to get out in the evenings because we were not sleeping well and we were exhausted. So we weren't seeing much of each other and that was causing its own problems. We hit on the idea about going out for breakfast after the kids had gone to school. It works really well, Si just goes into work later and we catch up.

Often to make looking after yourself a possibility you need to put in place the second priority.

Asking for help

Again I know I'm repeating myself but I don't think being a parent of a child with special needs was designed to be a one- or two-person job. Parenting works best as a community activity anyway; for parenting children with special needs it's essential. What you need to do is build up a network of support. Consider the following:

- You have to believe you need and deserve help if you're going to ask for it. Taking a long hard look at how stressful your life is, is a helpful place to start.

- If someone who you trust offers to have your child, take them up on it.

- Chase up social services and voluntary organisations for support.

- Sometimes friends and family find it hard to have your child, but they are happy to do some practical things like your ironing, or some shopping for you. Take them up on it.

- Look at getting a volunteer to help. Some areas have volunteer bureaus which will send someone to befriend your child or help you practically. Some national organisations like the National Autistic Society (see Resource directory for details) have a similar system. If you live near a university or college of further education, students are often interested.

Be gentle and kind to ourselves

We are often our own harshest critics; we give ourselves such a hard time. We will all react differently to stress – how we react depends on our previous life experiences, personality and emotional makeup. However, it's important to remember that, as with people who have lived through traumatic events, we live lives that make us more fragile and vulnerable to the effects of stress, so we need to be gentle and kind to ourselves.

Stop seeing letting things out as a weakness

It is not weak to admit to yourself how hard things are; in fact it makes all the difference. It is the start of dealing with stored up feelings that otherwise stop you thinking clearly about day-to-day situations.

It is very difficult to manage stress unless you do deal with these stored up feelings. Otherwise, despite wanting to get on with our lives, we get stuck. Further, without doing so can lead to aggression and depression that damage family life and relationships. In the next chapter we'll look more closely at this issue.

Become visible

As I've noted before, parents of children with disabilities have a strong tendency to become invisible. Becoming visible means letting people around you know how difficult your life can be, rather than letting them load yet more pressure on you.

Make connections

Very often, stress comes out first in how we feel physically. If we're aware of our weak spots, for example, headaches, uncomfortable stomach or backache, we can make the connection and we can start to deal with the stress. 'Could the fact I'm getting all these headaches be a result of all this stress?'

Information

We all need to be able to make sense of things. Part of this is knowing as much as possible about the condition of the child and how it could have happened.

☞   **My story**

When Jonathan and Carys were diagnosed I became an 'information junkie'. I wanted to know as much as possible about their condition. I became obsessed by the Internet.

Living with our child changes us: we react differently and feelings and emotions can feel really out of control. We find ourselves thinking things that we barely imagined were possible and often we give ourselves a really hard time about this. We need to understand how our changed thoughts, feelings and behaviours relate to the incredibly stressful experiences we are going through, and, that no matter how uncomfortable and problematic these are, they are normal.

Neglect

This is an odd heading for a book on parenting. But observations of others and myself cause me to believe that parents of children with disabilities need to learn the art of 'loving neglect'. When any child is born, they seem to deliver a large amount of guilt. When a child with special needs is born, the guilt is doubled. Often because of this we can feel guilty for neglecting him for a single moment. However, 'neglect' can often produce benefits: the child may be forced to develop new ways of doing things, he may have to rely on others and communicate to get his needs. Also, our other children need us. It is perfectly OK to 'neglect' your child with a disability from time to time in order to be good parents to your other children. Finally, neglect helps us to be good to ourselves. Parents need to recognise the importance of their partnership and especially not sacrificing their relationship for the sake of the child's care. We are also important; we have individual desires, dreams and hopes. The message is hold on to some of your dreams by a bit of loving neglect.

Let go of the expectations and pressures of performance-led parenting

Start to see parenting as being about developing safe places based on acceptance and love where children are allowed to be. Then children can develop in their own way. They can be who they are and you can be who you are. It's less stressful that way!

Afterthought

Talking about stress does not take it away. You still have to live your life, I still have to live mine. However, I think there's something really important about saying this is a shared reality for all of us. You're not on your own and somehow that is a good place to start – being connected to other people.

6 The emotional journey: facing the feelings

The way it is

Children have a habit of making you aware of feelings inside yourself that you had no idea existed, such as uncontrollable rage, sorrow or a deep sense of joy. This is true for all parents. For parents of children with disabilities the feelings we experience are even more intense and can be fairly constant.

> ☞ **My story**
>
> In the early stages of both of my children's diagnosis, if someone had said to me I was experiencing grief, I would have been both angry and ashamed. So desperate was I to prove to everyone how positive I felt about the whole experience. And yet beneath the smile there was an array of powerful emotions that were causing me turmoil. Now, three years later, I can express them best as those emotions that accompany grief; when someone dies.

In many ways it is wrong to put into words what parents of children with special needs feel. We are all individuals; we will all feel things differently. Yet many of us are sharing a similar experience. A teacher who I interviewed, who has worked with children with disabilities and their families for many years, observed:

> The impact of a child with special needs is huge; it is very stressful. Every parent has a dream for his or her child. When you realise those dreams are not going to come true, it can be devastating. It takes a long time. You wonder if you will ever get over it.

We often feel similar intense and painful feelings that can be compared to the way you feel when someone close to you dies. It is not the same but it is the nearest human experience. Looking at what we feel as a grief process gives us a way of understanding the chaos and turmoil of our feelings.

These feelings hit us all in different ways: some people feel one feeling at a time, others feel everything at once. Very often these feelings are revisited at different points. They don't have a beginning, middle or end.

This chapter is as usual, in two sections. This section, 'The way it is', considers each of the feelings in turn and the way it's likely to affect us. The next section, 'Moving on', looks at some of the reasons for why it really helps to face feelings and some ideas about how to deal with feelings.

Denial

Denial is the refusal inside you to believe what is happening. Refusal sums it up quite well. You just want to go on as if nothing has changed despite the increasing evidence to the contrary. A key issue about being in denial is that you refuse to admit you are in denial! It doesn't seem to matter who you are or what your past experience was.

> ### ☞ My story
>
> I was a family worker with a number of years of experience in child development. In one part of my mind, I knew that Jonathan was not developing in the usual way, but the other parts refused to accept it. 'He has language delay that's all; he's just a late developer.' I devised ways of not having to face reality such as avoiding typical children. At that point I was very isolated.
>
> Even after his diagnosis I still held back believing the whole truth. 'Well if he is autistic it's only mild.'

It came as a great relief to me to discover that this is a normal reaction. Shock and disbelief are really common responses to traumatic events in our lives. It actually serves a really important purpose. Our minds are processing very difficult information, as Robert Naseef (2001: 40) says '. . . denial buys us time to discover the inner strength to handle a problem.' It makes sense that only part of my mind could accept Jonathan's autism. I was naturally trying to protect myself and stop myself feeling overwhelmed. Even when the information has been mentally processed we still might not be able to accept the information emotionally. So we'll deny that we're upset about the news or that this problem will change our lives. Denial continues throughout our lives because the longing we have

> ### 📖 Parent's story
>
> Sometimes, I have a whole list of emotions in the same day. Maybe pride from him doing good work at school in the morning. Then, frustration because he won't eat his lunch, then embarrassment when I find out he's been badly behaved at school in the afternoon. And, finally anger as he lies on the pavement instead of walking home.

> ### 📖 Parents' story
>
> When we found out he had dyspraxia, at first I denied it.

as human beings to be like everyone else and for our family to be like every other family doesn't go away.

Anxiety and fear

Parent's story

I'm really worried and apprehensive about what he'll be like in the future.

These are the feelings most easy to spot. Anxiety and stress seem to go together; for many parents of children with disabilities anxiety is an everyday feeling. This is definitely true of me. If I listen to my body I'm hitting a fairly anxious state most days. I breathe faster, my heart rate goes up and I feel an edge of panic. To feel like this every day might seem an extreme thing to say, but if we consider the day-to-day stress many of us are under it should not be a surprise. There is not just daily stress but also future fear. It's always there at the back of your mind: 'How are we going to manage when he gets bigger?' A family support worker I interviewed put it really well: 'There is a no man's land of not knowing what the future will hold.'

Anxiety and fear can make us appear overprotective and very distracted. In the past I've been embarrassed to admit how anxious I've felt. It's a very uncomfortable feeling for others to deal with and people around you normally want to calm you down. However, not only are anxiety and fear normal in the circumstances that many of us live in, but it's our body's way of helping us cope. The truth is we need a lot of energy to look after our children and as we've seen before often we need to be hyper-vigilant. To do this, our bodies produce a lot of adrenalin to mobilise energy for what lays ahead and to anticipate problems, especially around danger, before they start – anxiety is the normal result of this. Fear is also a natural response to danger. It's our bodies way of giving us advance warning: you need to think about this before it happens. There is no denying the fact that our children may be in crisis situations, it will get harder as they get older and there will be battles ahead with services so our children can have their needs met. It's healthy to feel afraid; it's the springboard to problem solving.

Anger

Parent's story

Sometimes I get really angry, I take so much and then I just flip.

Parent's story

A lot of the time, I feel angry with myself and this makes me unhappy.

We all get angry but some of us, including me, find it very hard to admit that we are incredibly angry. It is one of the most intense and scariest feelings to deal with. If we do get angry, it's easier for the anger to be 'out there'. There are good and justifiable reasons to be angry at the society in which we live. Our children often do not get a fair deal, and fighting to change conditions for them is incredibly important, yet sometimes our anger is really a lot closer to home. We can feel angry with the child with special needs. If you're anything like me you'll do anything but admit to that.

I've spent a lot of years getting angry with myself, with Si, and even Carys has had anger directed at her; all anger I really felt for Jonathan. It is, somehow, socially unacceptable to own up to anger that at times feels like rage towards a little boy who does not mean to do the things he does, and yet who can cause chaos and mayhem. The middle of the night is the worst time for me. Rage is a frightening feeling. Si and myself have an agreement so when we feel like that the other one takes over – even if it's 2 a.m. in the morning.

The other part of anger is the rage against the universe. 'Why me?' and 'Why did this happen to me?' We are trying to make sense and process something that doesn't make sense. The universe seems unfair and it is reasonable to be bitter and very angry. The problem is some of us can get stuck here in the same way you can get stuck in depression. At this point anger can feel very isolating. The problem is not the anger itself but the getting stuck in a spiral of negative thoughts and feelings. Actual expressed anger can be very healthy: it can give you great energy and strength; it can enable you to work with your child; and it can help you function.

Guilt

Anger is pretty much always followed by guilt. It seems to me that most parents I've worked with feel guilty about their children, whether they are have special needs or not. The society we live in is a blame culture; everyone has high expectations of everyone else, so when things go wrong it has to be someone's fault. Very often parents are now blamed.

If you have a child with special needs the guilt is just more intense. It often starts before diagnosis. It's not unusual for parents to blame themselves for their child's disability.

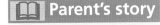

Parent's story

The main thing is guilt.
What did I do wrong?
The whole world revolves
around what you do
wrong.

> ☞ **My story**
>
> When Jonathan was a baby, I had mild post-natal depression. It wasn't paralysing, I could function fairly well but it was enough for me to believe that his lack of eye contact and lack of ability to gain speech was my fault. It was one of the reasons why I was frightened to get him checked out, in case they said it was me – that I was a bad parent.

The diagnosis process itself just makes guilt worse. We've already considered how it's often so focused on what is wrong with the child. Also, cultures from many parts of the world have a common view that bad things happen to bad people; the diagnosis makes you feel this is bad and it's your fault. The truth is events happen that are unjust and out of our control.

To add to this, our rage may be unexpressed but often it has caused us to think unimaginable things – hatred of our child's disability and hatred towards the child himself. The trouble with guilt, as we've seen previously, is that it freezes you up; there is a lot of self-doubt involved. It's hard to make decisions, and, crucially with our children, it's hard to lay boundaries down. When I feel like this I get into 'compensation culture', so for example, 'I've felt these terrible things about Carys, so it's OK if she stays up till 10 p.m.' Children with special needs often present you with situations that need clear thinking and problem solving; guilt makes it really hard to do these things. If it is not expressed over a number of years, guilt gets stored up. When you have been frozen up for a while you start to believe 'I'm not very good at being a parent.' Guilt is a normal, understandable reaction. The problem comes when it causes you to not react as you would normally and to believe things about yourself that are simply not true.

> ☞ **My story**
>
> I remember being really relieved when we were advised to put Jonathan on a special diet. I threw myself into finding him nice things to eat. In my head I was thinking, 'At last, something I can do for him.' My guilt had by then paralysed me so much that I actually believed there was nothing else I could do for him except bake cakes.

Shame

Shame is a very hidden feeling. It often follows guilt and the two are often confused, but shame is a deeper, more intense feeling. We have our own view of ourselves, we have our own ideals about how we should be. When things happen to us over which we have no control we fail those ideals. We feel ashamed. So we start off feeling intense rage, like hatred, towards our child. That hatred turns to guilt and the guilt, unless expressed, turns quickly to shame. It depends on our personalities and experiences as to how quick this process is. If we were made to feel ashamed as children on a regular basis, then shame as an adult happens quickly too.

Shame is a very powerful emotion that very often makes us feel terrible. But the problem with shame is that it makes us want to hide; we feel exposed and we want to cover up. The last thing we want to do is tell people how we really feel. The opposite happens and actually we put a lot of energy into warding people off. It depends on personality: some will attack other people; others will pretend, often quite beautifully, that everything is fine; some choose just to withdraw from everybody else; and others condemn themselves. At times I've done all these things.

> ☞ **My story**
>
> There was a long time, when I had a perfected smile – I could be enthusiastic, humorous and cheerful. I would even hear people say, 'You're really good with him, I don't know how you do it.' And then I'd come home and close the door and sit and watch him in his little world and just feel terrible.

If only fleetingly, many parents will at some point feel like this. It is a normal human emotion; it's just that we rarely if ever talk about it.

Sadness and grief

We will all feel sadness and grief differently. Some feel it quietly, an empty, hollow yearning for something that isn't there. For some it comes out in anger and frustration. Others feel it touched with depression.

> 📖 **Parent's story**
>
> There is pain in my heart. I ask myself, 'Why me? Why this situation, I came to this country to look for a better life not this.'

> 📖 **Parent's story**
>
> I wish I were dead sometimes.

Whichever way it comes it's accompanied by a lot of emotional pain, heartache and for many, anguish. Of all the feelings that parents feel, it is these feelings that mark you out as different. So why do we feel sad? Most of us will have had some sort of expectations before our children were born: what our child was going to be like; what they would grow up and develop into; our relationship with them; what family life would be like. When you receive that diagnosis, some part of that expectation is lost. At the root of our sadness is that loss. There is also day-to-day sadness and grief that other parents with typical children simply do not experience. Often our children have complex medical issues that cause them to be in pain. Sometimes society is unjust and unfair in the way it treats our children.

When you look at this sadness and grief, the way we feel is very like bereavement except in one crucial way – the person we grieve is still alive. This causes a great deal of problems. Not only do few people around us account for the fact that we might be grieving, but we feel guilty for feeling this way. This seems to be a grief that is not allowed.

Some of us stay with these feelings longer than others. Most of us revisit them time and time again. Like grief for someone who has died this is a personal process that will affect us individually:

the length of time, it's severity and the sequence will vary from person to person. Like traditional grief it will often affect us at unexpected moments.

> ☞ **My story**
>
> I saw a boy come out of school the other day who was in nursery with Jonathan. He was talking ten to the dozen, clutching a piece of writing he'd done that day. In nursery, it was much easier to convince myself that really there was little difference between him and Jonathan. But now as I stood watching the difference was striking between this boy and the one who would be soon dropped off in the white special needs' school minibus.

Also it's important to remember that, like traditional grief, this sadness and grief affected everyone – not just our other children, but also grandparents and other members of our extended family.

Acceptance

📖 Parent's story

At a point I had to come to terms with the problem and decide to accept it.

For many people acceptance is not a feeling but a decision. Also it's often a struggle. Acceptance is about letting go of our preconceived ideas of not just our child but how we see our lives turning out. Some of us find that harder than others. There are many factors involved. It depends on your background and childhood and also on the severity of the child's disability. Both Si and myself found it harder to let go of our expectations of Carys, who is quick, verbal and intelligent, but has difficulties, than we did of Jonathan whose disability is more profound.

Once you make the choice to accept, the most obvious feelings are relief and release. Life feels easier to manage. My personal observation is that acceptance is when things start to turn around. It has the result of clearing a space in your head and reducing the effects of guilt and shame. It becomes possible to plan and problem solve the present and future.

📖 Parent's story

You can feel elated for things that other people take for granted.

The best benefit though is the way you start to look at the world and appreciate your children in an entirely different way. Our value systems begin to change and we start to realise what our children give us, not what they are taking away. Micheline Mason (2000: 21) makes the point that disabled people give us the 'gift of slowness'. In our society, life now runs at ridiculous speeds, which are unhealthy and cause us high degrees of stress. Everything we do has to have a productive end or an outcome. So we stop doing the things that would improve the quality of our lives, such as long conversations with friends, appreciating nature or just thinking.

☞ My story

My children make me slow. Carys needs things explained slowly, so she can process what is going on. It takes time, sometimes we need to draw it. Often, we have to talk about how we feel. We have long conversations and without realising it our relationship is enriched.

It takes a long time to walk with Jonathan. He likes to feel every texture on every wall. He likes to examine the ground underneath him and he loves trees. I used to stand there bored while he paused to look at one of his trees. Jonathan does not like to be dragged away when there is a tree to look at. One day I looked to see what he was looking at. I saw light streaming through leaves in a shimmery way. It was beautiful but until my son showed it to me, I'd never noticed.

Moving on

Ideas

We live in a society that is not very good at managing feelings. Gone are the days of the traditional 'British stiff upper lip', but society would still prefer feelings to be sorted out quickly and cleanly, then swept out of the way.

Unfortunately, feelings are messy. They can stay around and make life uncomfortable for you and the people around you. A common reaction is to try and side step this by doing something, taking action to sort your problems out. However, without dealing with feelings, problems are much harder to solve.

Facing feelings: why it helps

- It's practical

  Looked at from a fairly matter-of-fact level if you want to deal with difficulties at home and just simply get on with your life, feelings need to be faced, felt and expressed.

- Without dealing with feelings it's hard to meet our needs

  We've already seen how intense and often traumatic these feelings are. To switch off or bottle up feelings takes a lot of energy, which means that there's nothing left to deal with the rest of your life in a constructive way.

- Without dealing with feelings, we hurt people

  We don't mean to, but to protect ourselves from how we feel, we harm others. We do it not just by lashing out in anger but also by withdrawing and detaching ourselves. Very often, it's the people we love that bear the brunt of this.

- Not dealing with feelings leads to health problems

  Feelings have to go somewhere; if they're not expressed they will come out in physical symptoms – being run down, ill, as well as anxiety-related conditions such as high blood pressure and breathing difficulties.

- We can't teach our children to manage their emotions if we don't deal with ours

  As we've considered previously the ability to handle our emotions and get on with people (emotional intelligence) is very important. Children learn a great deal from what they see you doing.

Dealing with feelings: ways that help

- Connect

  Feelings often start physically so your body is a good place to start finding your feelings. For example, when I'm anxious, my chest feels tight and when I'm angry, my head feels tight and I get hot.

- Accept feelings as natural

  Allow yourself time to feel what you feel. Accept that these feelings have a natural course. Holding back the feelings means the process of coming to terms with what's going on just takes longer.

- Respect your feelings

  Recognise that your feelings are important and valuable. The feelings are reminding you of the difficult events that you've been through.

- Learn to forgive yourself

  One of the hardest things to do is to forgive ourselves. There are many things we regret and are not proud of, but if we punish ourselves forever we can't move on. Forgiveness means letting go. Understanding why things have happened is important. Very often at the time we were under huge pressure and had little support. I find it very helpful to reflect that I am often doing the best I can with the limited resources available to me.

- Learn from your children

  Most children have no problems telling you how they feel – be it using words, sounds or behaviour. Also they can be delightfully forgiving.

- Let it out

  Do what you need to do to express emotions. Big boys and girls cry and it's good for them. Tears are very therapeutic and so is a good scream. Often people need to do something physical when they're angry. Whatever you need to do make it a priority to do it.

- Look after yourself

  Give yourself some time every day that is for looking after you. Within reason and when you have choice, try to do what's good for you for a longer time at least once a week. This might mean giving yourself permission to withdraw and vegetate, or go out and have a laugh without feeling guilty.

- Forgiving others

  I know not everyone is going to agree but giving up resentment and often hatred and forgiving others is a process that helps

some people towards moving on. This is not to say that our anger and bitterness is not utterly justified. Extremely unjust things happen to our children and us. Fighting for justice is important. Yet for many of us to move on, letting go is important.

Practical support ideas

■ Find some caring, sensitive and gentle people and be with them

I know I've said this before but having 'listeners' is really helpful. Parents of children with disabilities need to have people who will acknowledge their feelings as really significant rather than trying to play them down. We don't need advice, clichés or people who problem solve without listening to your feelings first. So anyone who starts their sentence 'If I were you I'd . . .' or 'Cheer up, everything will work out' may be worth avoiding at this point in your life.

■ If you get stuck in how you feel see a counsellor

Some people find short-term counselling to be really helpful if you feel unable to move on.

■ Play football or any sport

Si (enthusiastically) and I (reluctantly) concede that playing football has been a really beneficial way of him dealing with some of his feelings. Joking apart, exercise can be a really important way of managing feelings.

Afterthought

I think maybe this chapter should have a health warning. Delving into feelings can be a scary thing and yet if we are to live a good enough life I think it is something worth doing.

Here are some observations about facing the feelings:

■ This is a journey – there are no timetables; it just takes as long as it takes;

■ These reactions are normal; most people go through at least some of them;

■ Start being a person not just a parent;

■ Take care of your body;

■ Lean on your spirituality;

■ Explain to others what you need rather than waiting for others to guess.

Families

The way it is

> ☞ **Professional's comment**
>
> Parents learn a lot about themselves; families learn a lot about themselves.

> ☞ **Professional's comment**
>
> It can often affect the social life of a family: can become a loss for the whole family, can't have holidays, not invited to people's houses. You end up being ruled by your child with special needs.

A child with a disability can affect the people around him profoundly, positively and negatively. This chapter takes a closer look at what it's like to live in a family with a child with special needs from the point of view of mothers, fathers, brothers and sisters. This section, 'The way it is' considers some of the experiences of family members that are rarely spoken about and the next section 'Moving on' looks at ideas and strategies that help a family survive.

Dads

I'm really grateful for the contributions of Si, my husband for this section.

Dads and diagnosis

The roles of mums and dads have changed over the last few years as more and more women have returned to work. Generally, however, especially when the child is young, fathers are still more likely to be

> 📖 **Parent's story**
>
> I don't describe my home life as normal. I can't sit down and relax because of the children. Imran doesn't sleep, so that means there's not enough sleep for the whole family.

> 📖 **Parent's story**
>
> Meal times are hard because if he doesn't like the food he throws it on the floor or on someone else's plate.

> 📖 **Parent's story**
>
> It took my partner a long time to accept that there is something wrong with Thomas.

> 📖 **Parent's story**
>
> Initially my husband would go away and leave me with Becky. I think that was the shock. But we're closer now. He's more involved and has changed towards Becky.

out at work and thus have less daily contact with their child. This can mean that the process of coming to terms with the diagnosis can take the following pattern:

■ A lot of men will have high expectations, especially of their sons. If diagnosis happens in the early years of life, they are more likely to deny there is a problem for a longer period of time.

■ After the diagnosis, it seems that everything is focused on the mum and child. To the dad it can feel that his needs are being ignored and yet his feelings are just as intense. As everyone around them just expects them to cope, that's what they try and do.

■ At this stage a common reaction is for men to bury themselves at work and be very focused on practical issues such as long-term financial care for the child and they will be less involved in caring responsibilities. Very often this changes and they start to look after the child more. With the change, they also begin to process what's happened and begin to take in the implications of life after diagnosis.

■ When they do process and come to terms with it, it can hit them very hard. I wonder whether women, being with the child every day, have time to slowly adapt, whereas for men, it can be more of a shock.

Fathers and emotions

> ☞ **Si's story**
>
> How do I feel about Jono? – confused, angry, elated, despairing, amused and entertained, frustrated, overwhelmed (sometimes by joy, sometimes despair!), and mainly so glad that he is part of my life. I love him intensely, while wondering if he may tip me over the edge into insanity.

In many ways, Si and I feel exactly the same about our experience of having Jonathan as a son. The difference is in the way we express our emotions. There are far more barriers for men to actively express sadness. Where there is any family crisis, there is often a high expectation that they will look after everyone else and take charge of the practical details. Quite recently a father who had just found out his child has autism told me that his GP had told him that he must be strong and look after his wife. This was despite the fact that he was feeling just as shocked and grief stricken as she was. These sort of expectations, spoken or unspoken, mean that for a dad to express how he feels takes a lot of effort and bravery.

 **Si's story**

As a man and a father, even in our more enlightened 21st century, society is a hard place to be. Allowing your emotions out (and it is a roller-coaster of ups and downs with Jono), finding support, or even admitting that you need to find support, is still not easy.

Dads and parenting

 **Si's story**

Being Jono's dad has revolutionised my ideas about parenting, my ability to cope with pressure and a lack of sleep, and taught me how unnecessary conventions, such as shoes and socks and knives and forks, really are.

When a child with a disability arrives, both men and women can have a revolution in their ideas about parenting. The difficulty for men is they have less space, time and opportunity to discuss what is going on than women do. Some men are naturally very practical by nature and can have an inbuilt desire to fix things for their partner and children. One of the most difficult issues is coming to terms with the fact that their child with a disability is not a situation they can fix.

There is also the issue of the chaos that living with a child with special needs can bring to your home life.

 **Si's story**

For someone who likes everything tidy, returning to complete chaos in the house often means taking a deep breath and remembering why it's like this – searching the garden by torchlight for the missing back door key certainly makes for an interesting evening.

Dads and work

If there are two people involved in parenting a child, in the majority of cases, one of them has to work. Commonly it is the dad who has the full-time job. This can put a great deal of hidden pressure on dads.

> ☞ **Si's story**
>
> The pressures of juggling work and home are intensified by the unreal demands that home sometimes has. Often I will drag myself into work, having not had enough sleep and struggling to function, but it's still easier than being at home.

The importance of fathers

In a family where there is a child with a disability fathers are so much more than providers and protectors. In the 'Positively Parents' study (Beresford 1994) dads were regarded by those interviewed as the most significant emotional support for mothers, who in this study were the full-time carers. The sense that I utterly share is that mums and dads are in this together. To get through the experience mutually supporting each other really is the only option.

Mums

In the main in this country, as in many others, mothers are the ones who stay at home with the children. As we have seen, because mums are more concerned with the daily care of the child, often the process of coming to terms with the diagnosis will happen quicker for them.

Parent's story

It's very painful. Blessing scratches her friends and it's very hard to see them running away from her. And then she's not invited to birthday parties.

In the beginning, a common reaction to the diagnosis is to just give up any ideas of doing anything else with your life except bringing up this child with a disability. I can clearly remember thinking after Jonathan had been diagnosed, 'That's it then, no career for me.' However, eventually that solution doesn't work for everyone anymore. Women begin to hanker after freedom. Practically, mothers become exhausted and at their wits end; emotionally, their self-esteem goes down rapidly; and socially they are feeling very isolated. As the child grows older, the mother's world grows smaller. Mums start asking 'Who can I be friends with?' It's very difficult to relate to those parents who have children of his own age but also it's hard to relate to those who have younger children. So, the mum's relationships become limited to those people who accept the child's disability.

Mothers and emotional needs

In many cultures a common image of women, especially mothers, is one of sacrifice and denial of her own needs and wants so that she can take care of others. If you are brought up to believe that looking after others is your highest duty then often you will have learned how to ignore your own needs. This often causes real problems for mums who have a child with a disability. For example:

- We sometimes don't know what our own needs are

  We have already seen how crucial it is when you are a parent of a child with a disability to look after yourself, but the first step has to be to find out what you need. This can be hard if it goes against the way you were brought up. Thus it's really important to spend time listening to yourself.

- We have problems expressing our needs

  Often we express our needs in such a way that it sounds as if our needs are unimportant and we're apologising for them.

☞ My story

I used to apologise, ask permission and make excuses when I wanted something: 'I'm really sorry but is it all right if I go and read my book for a bit? It's just that I've had the kids all day . . .'. Whereas Si is much more likely to say 'I'm going to have 10 minutes on the computer.' I'm learning to be clearer and not make a big deal about it. So now I'll try to say: 'I need some time out so I'm going to read my book for a bit.'

Couples

☞ Our story

Sustaining a relationship is one of the hardest pressures, and after meeting the needs of the kids there is often little left. Honesty and hard work are probably the only things to keep going with some days . . . or weeks . . . or at its worst months.

There is no conclusive research about what a child with a disability does to a couple's relationship. Like any other stressful event it can bring people together or drive people apart.

Positive benefits

Parenting a child where the parenting rulebook seems to have been thrown away and where daily demands are extraordinary is, as

Parent's story

It's not really a partnership anymore, we are just there for the children. My husband feels as though he's left out because of the kids' behaviour.

we've seen, stressful and traumatic, but often couples find connections within each other that they didn't know were there. It can develop increased closeness and strength in a relationship. Very often, you have to work at it; crisis situations mean that little will happen on its own. However, the working through things often brings deeper understanding and sometimes more intimacy than would have been expected if circumstances had been more normal. Your respect for the other person often grows as you see them coping with what you know is incredible pressure. You often make sacrifices for each other, which in the life you're living are huge.

☞ Our story

In our case this is always about giving the other one a lie-in or, if you're feeling really saintly, a whole extra night's sleep.

Dangers

In Chapter 5 we noted that the sort of stress parenting a child with a disability causes is like no other, in that it is ongoing with no beginning, middle or end. Most other crises that hit a couple's relationship, such as a bereavement or unemployment, happen in an intense period of time. There is much potential for conflict and difficulties in the relationship.

Early issues

One of the most dangerous stages for the relationship is right at the beginning, soon after diagnosis. The reality is that some relationships break down at this point. There can be a number of reasons for this:

- One partner cannot accept the news, unwilling to make the sacrifice of time and energy for the child.

- Those with fragile and unstable relationships to start with can often not take the pressure.

- Different emotional reactions – We have already seen how a child with a disability can cause intense emotions to occur in parents: shame, inadequacy, loss of self-control, self-doubt and sadness to name but a few. However, we have also seen that men and women experience and express emotions differently and may not feel the same emotions at the same time. So, there is much room for misunderstanding and conflict. Also it's really tempting to take out your negative feelings on each other, each partner blaming the other. Another reaction is to withdraw from each other completely, which can be equally destructive.

Negative patterns

If these reactions go on over a long period of time, negative patterns can appear. At the root of it are the child's continued demands that can swamp the relationship. Matters can be made worse if the child with a disability becomes the focus for everything; all the energy, attention, creativity and love can go into the child, and what's left is reserved for other children, leaving precious little for the parents' relationship. A common pattern is for the dad to feel excluded. Meetings and appointments for the child happen during the day, if the mother is the main carer it is very hard for the dad to keep taking time off. Therefore he is effectively out of the information loop and isolated. If the mum's focus is exclusively on the child this isolation just increases.

Being single

Single parent families are obviously under continual greater stress than families where there are two parents. If you then add a child with a disability to the picture, the situation can look very difficult.

- Being one person means life can be incredibly lonely and frustrating. There is no obvious person to problem solve with, so it's easier to worry, become very anxious or angry and lose perspective.

- Life can be utterly exhausting because as well as all the normal tasks involved in running a household, there are all the medical needs, like incontinence, to deal with, not to mention all the sleepless nights.

- Everyday life can become one set of tasks after another set of tasks. It is all very serious, the idea of having fun and a laugh are far away.

- Not only are you dealing with the enormous implications of having a child with special needs, but also with the intense feelings that often come after the break-up of a relationship, which is often like a bereavement in itself. All this on your own.

It's completely natural in these circumstances to feel like giving up and at the very least to become fatalistic and stop fighting.

Brothers and sisters

Positive benefits

Other children can bring normality to a family experiencing abnormal events. Being a parent to them is more straightforward; you don't have to rewrite the rules in quite the same way. Brothers and sisters have natural wants and desires too, which force the family to do normal activities and therefore make the family less isolated.

They also help parents tremendously with their child with special needs. They are often great role models and can be patient and sensitive playmates for the child with a disability. Often a child with special needs can have the effect of bringing a family together. Brothers and sisters can feel as though they are part of a team, with a sense not only of belonging but also of meaning and purpose. This can give them good feelings about themselves in terms of their self-esteem and identity (Sullivan 1979). Finally, other children are really good at reminding us that our child with a disability is first of all a child. They see a brother or sister, not a label.

Dangers

I am grateful to two people for this section: Donald Meyer author of *Sibshops* (1994) who has written about family relationships and especially brother and sister relationships in a family where there is a disability and the unique perspective of my daughter Carys.

Meyer makes the point that although brothers and sisters of children with disabilities are just like any other children, there are some unique differences. Some of these issues will now be discussed.

Can I catch it?

Brothers or sisters can worry that they might catch or share their brother with special needs' condition. 'Can I catch autism?', 'When will my epilepsy begin?' This is particularly true in younger children, who believe in magic and don't really understand the difference between an illness like chicken-pox and conditions like cerebral palsy. 'If I caught chicken-pox I can catch cerebral palsy.'

Brothers and sisters need accurate information about their sister's disabilities; things that are obvious to adults are not to children. Yet so often in the diagnosis process, the brothers and sisters are completely overlooked.

Embarrassment

There are many reasons why brothers and sisters can feel embarrassed. For example:

- The whole family gets looked at or even spoken to in public places because of the child with special needs' behaviour.

- The fact that the child with a disability looks different.

- When a brother or sister has a hidden disability they can act in strange, bizarre ways.

 **Carys' story**

We were in a restaurant on holiday and Jonathan started screaming. The people behind us started looking at us. I didn't look at him because I felt so embarrassed. Even though I'm used to it, it still felt really horrible.

Shame

If you put guilt and embarrassment together you get shame. And shame as we've noted in Chapter 6 is a difficult emotion for adults to deal with and express and therefore that much harder for children. Brothers and sisters can feel that their family is now 'marked'. If children are never encouraged to express their negative feelings they will carry them to adult life. It can cause them to make choices in adult life that are driven by shame and guilt. It is worth noting that where there are only two children in a family, one with special needs and one that is atypical, these guilt feelings are much more likely to occur.

Fear

 **Carys' story**

Sometimes when Jonathan is having a tantrum you don't look like my mum and dad because you don't know what to do.

This point made by Carys shows her insight into the situation. Even cool nine-year-olds have a strong belief that parents always know what to do in any event. So when they are faced with a situation with their brother or sister which is clearly out of a parent's control the children like Carys can feel really frightened and confused. This is not how life is supposed to be.

They can become a 'parental child'

The feeling of chaos and being out of control can cause some children to take on responsibilities way beyond their years. Although in one way this can encourage new skills and independence, the danger is that it can stop them enjoying the freedom of childhood.

Not getting enough attention

As a parent, I know that Jonathan will at times get far more attention than Carys. The reason is simple: his needs are more severe. Yet brothers and sisters' problems can be as serious as those of the child with special needs, they are just not so immediate. The danger is that as parents we overlook their struggles and also their achievements. We do this not only at the cost of our children's happiness but also at the long-term cost of family relationships. 'Good' children now can become resentful teenagers and adults.

Moving on

Ideas and strategies

Dads

For this section I am indebted to 'Fathers – Are we meeting their needs?' (Carpenter and Herbert 1997). The research on dads of children with special needs is very limited indeed but what there is shows the following points can help dads move on.

- They like a practical way of being involved with their child

  In the main dads much prefer having a specific task as a way of getting involved with their child. At school that might be the sports day or fund raising. At home that might be taking the child swimming or teaching them how to do something.

- They need to be in the information loop as much as possible

  If it is not possible to take time off work for appointments during the day, there are other ways of achieving this. There are often weekend workshops organised by different organisations and it's good to attend such things together. The Internet, as we have noted, is a great source of information. Gathering information for a particular task is a really good way to be involved for men. It is noticeable that when there is a task, such as a complaint or a report for a special needs panel, it is often Si who does it.

- They need to move from distant wage earner to a more hands-on role

  Very often dads view themselves as the 'outsider'. Mums particularly can change that view by being clearer in their communication, especially when there is information to discuss and in expressing their needs and emotions. It's important not to assume that just because someone lives with you they know what is going on.

- They need to find a way to express their emotions in a way that works for them

  Sometimes men get to anger before any other emotion and often, whatever the emotion is, they need an active way to express it. This may be something physical like football or going out for a drink with a mate.

Mums

For mums there are two strategies to consider that can help them move on:

- Developing a life outside of being a mum

  In the long run, it is the degree to which this desire for freedom is sorted out which is the key to how enjoyable future life becomes. Some women successfully get dads, other members of their family and social services to help them do at least some of the things they want to do.

- Learning how to express needs in a productive way

  This is about learning how to communicate assertively, without blaming anybody, being aggressive or feeling guilty. We will return to this subject in the next chapter.

Couples

☞ **Professional's comment**

Where it works, parents work as a team.

Ideas and strategies to help couples move on include:

- Putting the relationship first

  I hear a hollow laugh from Si, let alone anyone else. There seems to be so little time for a relationship in the chaos of all the needs and demands of the home. I think that like looking after yourself, it has to be a belief system: 'We are going to put this relationship first no matter what.' When you develop that attitude, you'll snatch any opportunity you have and you will carve out time for each other.

- Learning to talk to each other about how you feel

  Very often things have to change in order for the relationship to work. Deeper understanding and connections need to be found between partners. The way through is to talk, work through painful feelings and come to some joint decisions.

- Both being involved in 'hands-on' parenting

  Both being involved 'hands on' in caring for your child with special needs is good for everyone.

- Having some fun together

  It's really important for parents to have an enjoyable time together, doing something special for them. Yet it is often rare that they do so. Having a laugh and doing non-parent activities together is so important.

- Rethinking communication

  Men and women may feel the same way over many key issues but as we have seen they express themselves very differently. There is a lot of space for misunderstanding and rows because of the stress couples in this position are under. So try to communicate clearly. If it helps use the ideas in Chapter 3 'Communication and relationship building' for describing what you want and need. Never assume that your partner will just understand what you need; you have to tell them!

- Being kind

  It's important to keep reminding each other how much stress you're under. Also have a few rules concerning relating to each other, such as try not to take your stress out on each other and try not to be critical of each other. There are ways of telling each other what you need without resorting to negativity.

Single parents

For single parents it is particularly important to consider the following points.

- Network with other parents

  You need other adults to communicate with and to have fun with, so, network with people you know and build up a support network as a matter of urgency. A circle of support is a good option to consider, see the next chapter for details.

- Look after yourself

  It is even more important that single parents spend time looking after themselves than probably any other group of parents. Don't postpone looking after yourself as it's a matter of basic safety because you can't be any help to your child unless you take care of yourself.

  - Be kind to yourself and be proud of what you're achieving;
  - Find out what options are available and access as much support as you can quickly;
  - Make that first call – It is always really difficult to ask for help but no one is going to come to you and offer help and make decisions for you. You can have control back by making some changes and looking at options.

- Know yourself

  Understand your limits, particularly when you can feel yourself going under and do something about it. Also, learning how to say 'no' to other people's demands is really important.

Brothers and sisters

There are a number of ideas that can help siblings move on. For example:

- Practical solutions

  Is there something that can be changed to reduce their embarrassment and help the child with a disability at the same time? For example, having a realistic view about going out as a family.

- Give the brother or sister space

  This is especially true of teenagers. Space gives them control; 'You don't have to walk with us.' Hand the agenda over to them, let them do it their way.

- Allowing other children to express their feelings

  If you can let them say how they feel, without being judged for it, whether those feelings are embarrassment, anger or even hatred, it will make a huge difference. They need to talk about their feelings and fears, to be reassured that it is OK to get angry and resentful at the amount of attention she gets.

  It's also good to say how you feel too: 'She is difficult to live with sometimes.' – this reflects reality. Finally, when there is a conflict between a brother or sister and the child with special needs see if they can work it out themselves. If brothers and sisters are not allowed to get angry or tease the child with a disability it will go underground and become stored up anger. They should be allowed to work out their conflicts as best they can, as long as it doesn't result in physical harm.

- Time

  It is important that they have time alone without any responsibilities; they want privacy and time with their friends; they want laughter and fun. Also they want time alone with their parents to talk and they want a relationship based on them as an individual.

- Information

  Good clear communication with their parents and information about the child with special needs is the best way of reducing their fears, anxiety and anger. It is in fact one of the best ways of helping them not become the 'parental child'.

Establishing a good family life

When I was researching this chapter, I was able to find a lot of research (Bristol 1984: 299; McCubbin and Patterson 1981; Darley *et al.* 2002) that showed what it was that enabled some families to cope and adapt to having a child with a disability, while other families felt overwhelmed. What I discovered was that it depended on the resources within the family for managing in a crisis. There are certain family characteristics that make a family more able to manage in a family crisis and more likely to get through and move on afterwards. These are:

1 Having a close-knit supportive home environment – Pulling together and working well as a team and being committed to helping and supporting each other within the family were all likely to make a close-knit and supportive home. This was more likely to happen if you did things with your children and worked on your relationship with your partner.

2 Being able to express feelings openly – It is important that everyone in the family is encouraged to act openly and honestly and to say how they feel without fear of being blamed.

3 Being actively involved in social and leisure activities outside the home with people outside the immediate family – Having relationships which make you feel valued is very important but also it's really important to have an identity outside of being a mum or dad.

Afterthought

This chapter gives us the beginnings of hope. The thought that it is possible to live a good life despite the incredible pressures we are often under within our family situations. That not only can a family survive but the people within it could grow and develop.

8 Hope

The way it is

Throughout this book my intention has been to try to be realistic but hopeful. I believe, despite everything we've looked at, that hope is not just possible but crucial to parenting a child with special needs. This is not a soft option; it's actually easier to give up than to keep on hoping. At a conference I attended I heard Raul Kaufman from the Options Institute talk about how he and his colleagues have been criticised for offering parents 'false hope'. He said there is no such thing as 'false hope' just 'hope'. What I'm suggesting here is not hope for a miracle cure, but realistic hope to believe in your child's capacity to grow and develop, and that you and your family can lead good and fulfilling lives. Such hope is powerful; it drives all your beliefs about yourself and your child. It actually affects your child's development, the choices you make in the present and the future plans you have for you and your family. There are many barriers to a hopeful future and a fulfilling present – many we've considered already. It's hope that ultimately gives you the power to break through those barriers.

This section, 'The way it is', looks at the factors that can cause us as parents to feel hopeful; they are as many and varied as we are. The first part focuses on our children, the second, on us as individuals. The next section, 'Moving on', looks at ways of breaking through the barriers that stop us hoping. It does so in two ways, firstly by considering some skills that will equip us and secondly by looking at some actions we can start to take.

Our children bring hope

To my surprise, when people observe our family the common reaction is distance and pity, particularly when they see Jonathan. A typical comment is one of respectful pity: 'I don't know how you do that, I wouldn't be able to cope.' This is a common reaction even among people who research families like mine. It's firmly entrenched in the Medical Model – our children are not normal so our families can't be and, even worse than that, the usual family bonds and emotions can't exist in our families. Stand back for a moment and think of the implications of this. The assumptions are that:

- Parents could not really love children who looked and behaved strangely.
- Our children could never be a source of joy.

The truth is this does not take account of the 'enormous role that feelings and emotions play in maintaining family life' (Beresford 1994: 67). That is the real clue to not just how a family survives living with a child with special needs but how they can live a good life. It is this simple; we love our children and our children themselves bring us hope.

They lift our spirits simply by being themselves

Our children often have wonderful unique personalities that make them attractive and endearing. Many are loving and affectionate. Some have innocence and such a pure spirit there's something quite incredible about being around them. Often they have a different way of looking at the world that is really refreshing and a lot less complicated than the one we have. Most of all they make us laugh.

> ### ☞ My story
>
> If I reflect on today, like most days, my favourite moments have been with my kids. There was Carys who brought me a fruit salad she'd made herself and then curled up beside me saying 'I won't talk because I know you're doing the book,' and then talked non-stop about her day. Then there was Jonathan, who never asks permission but just launches himself on me; he rearranged me three times so I was in the correct position to stroke his back while he ate his crisps. These are only moments out of a day with a lot of stress and difficulty, but they are the moments that shine.

Parent's story

Usman can be very loving, he can have a very intelligent conversation with you if you keep things plain and simple.

Parent's story

I think my little girl is loving, affectionate, content and caring. No matter what, she sings and makes me laugh.

Parent's story

I have to laugh at some of the things Jake has done.

They are likeable and other people are drawn to them

Very often when we are going through real battles with our children and can only see how difficult it is to be with them, others will say to us, 'Oh she was really well behaved,' or 'I love having him,' and really appear to mean it. Mystifying though it can be, I'm learning to see these as hopeful signs. It means that there will be people out there for my children who actually enjoy them at times when I'm really struggling.

They cope and overcome their disability

Parent's story

Sophie never lets anything stop her or hold her back. She gets on with everything. She has courage.

Many of our children do not see their disability, unless someone tells them they can't do something. They just see what they want to do and so often their determination and courage is breathtaking. They have a way of compensating and managing to get past barriers to where they want to be. In addition some of our children suffer a lot of physical pain as part of their normal day, often with little comment.

It's worth reflecting on the everyday ways our children challenge their labels and find ways for themselves of living good lives.

They have successes and achievements

Parent's story

I'm so proud when he achieves anything.

Our children's successes and achievements should be celebrated as more than anything they bring great hope. I know my friends' eyes glaze over when I say, 'You'll never guess what Jonathan did yesterday . . .'. The only defence I can make for my excitement is that we have waited a long time for many of the things Jono is now doing. Somehow that makes them more precious. I'm also aware of times when Carys does things that for other children would be no big deal but for her are a major achievement.

They surprise us

Our children always have a way of surprising us because first and foremost they are children. They seem to work on extremes. They can horrify and overwhelm us by how difficult their behaviour can be and the next minute amaze us by doing something extraordinary. They simply refuse to be 'put into a box' or stereotyped.

We can bring ourselves hope

I've tried to identify here some of the factors that cause us to feel hopeful and give us strength. Everyone is different so each person will find different factors that bring hope.

Being a parent

Some of us enjoy being a parent and despite everything find it satisfying. Perhaps there is also the growing realisation that we are doing something that we know others would find really hard and we are doing it well. We have discovered new ways of doing things.

Looking after yourself

I know I've laboured the point endlessly but how we care for ourselves is key to hope and strength as parents. Below are some possibilities.

Managing how you feel

Putting priority on looking after your feelings and what's going on for you underneath is an important way of maintaining hope and strength. To keep going we need a good perspective. If we don't keep a check on how we feel, things such as anxiety and depression can overwhelm us. We need to accept that these things will come because a lot of the time we're really tired and having to deal with a very demanding life. It's really important to know your limits, to know the early signs of things being too much for you. There is no shame or guilt in this; we are not superhuman. Also it's essential that you are honest with those around you about what is going on as soon as you can find someone to talk to.

> **📖 Parent's story**
>
> I've learnt to read the signs of when I'm losing the plot.

Avoid centring your life on your child

This is a change in how you think about yourself and your life; it's about putting your needs higher up the agenda. The major result is to make you feel more of a person and less of a parent of a child with special needs. How it works in practice varies from person to person. It might mean swimming once a week, an art class, football training or it might mean going back to work.

> **☞ My story**
>
> I'm fortunate in having a really flexible and tolerant employer and the fact that I was able to work even in the early days with Jonathan saved my sanity. At home it was wall-to-wall chaos but at work there were coffee breaks and tasks that I actually achieved. And it gave me something else to think about apart from autism.

Self-indulgence

The fact is that most of us have very little time to ourselves and it's hard on a day-to-day level to find large amounts of time. So use what you have well, savour it and snatch what comes to you unexpectedly not for the ironing but for you.

- Have particular treats at the end of the day;
- Lie in when you get the opportunity;

- Grab free time with your partner;
- Have a rest in the middle of the day.

> ☞ **My story**
>
> As it's hard for me right now to do big things that I'd like to do, I've developed the idea of doing small things well. So breakfast at the weekend is a real ritual: I plan ahead, it's always good coffee and perhaps croissants and always the paper.

Be creative

Parent's story

I play and listen to music.

Using your creative skills serves as an outlet for your feelings and helps you make sense of things. Whatever you do, from music to making things to writing things down, it can help give meaning, increases your confidence and can help you feel powerful again as a parent. Often because they are activities you do with others it also makes you feel less lonely and isolated.

Relationships

In previous chapters we've considered the importance of relationships in our lives. They are definitely key to hope, strength and feeling powerful about our own lives. A danger to parents of children with a disability is isolation. Below is a summary of some of the ideas about relationships we've already considered and some new suggestions.

- Start to think actively about becoming interdependent

  Develop a network of people in your life who have different roles: some practical like babysitters and some emotional like listeners. (This idea is developed further in the 'Moving on' section of this chapter.)

- Join a support group

  This has all sorts of benefits; people who understand who are in the same position as you, access into other networks that provide support and resources and very often a chance to unwind and have a good laugh.

- Join an email forum

  For many reasons, some people find it hard to join groups but the Internet is also a great way of meeting people in the same situation as you.

- Become involved in changing things for children with special needs in your community

  When you live something 24/7 with a child, being able to influence and ultimately change services for families and children brings increased feelings of self-worth and more control and power back to you as a parent. It also again brings you into contact with people of like mind. This might be through a local inclusion group or a parent partnership network.

- If you have a partner, value the relationship and put some time into it

  We mentioned in Chapter 7, 'Families', that a partner's support was crucial to a parent's well-being. If you never see each other you're never going to enjoy the benefits of that.

Attitudes and beliefs

Rethinking your beliefs and attitudes is a key part of discovering and holding on to hope and strength. In previous chapters we looked at how important it was when dealing with our children to believe that, 'I can make a difference here.' This is an ongoing process, doubts creep in all the time, and things people say knock us back. Keeping your confidence about what you're doing with your child is central to everything else that happens. Many of us have found our faith has an important part to play here.

There are other attitudes about life itself that can really help as well. Much of this is about rethinking and cutting free from the expectations that others and society place on us.

Home life

There is nothing that removes hope quicker than being overwhelmed by everything you have to do at home. To avoid this as much as possible get everyone in the family involved and pulling their weight. In this way you move from the position where you do everything to one where things are shared out. For example:

- Encourage the child with special needs to be involved

  No matter how severe your child's disability is they do not have to be completely helpless. They can still learn activities that make your life easier.

- Get your partner involved

Parents' stories

- I look into my mirror and say to myself, 'I can do it.'
- When something good happens with him, no matter how small, I tell myself, 'Well, think how hard things are for you, that was amazing.'
- I need to keep remembering that I know more about her than they do.

Parents' stories

- If it stresses me out, it goes.
- I decide what I want and what I can and can't live without.
- If you keep on about things that you're worried about they tend to enlarge in your head (Beresford 1994: 91).
- I don't care what people expect sometimes.

> ☞ **My story**
>
> Jonathan understands what 'tidy-up time' means. Although it's more work for me at the moment I'm making him clear up with me when he makes a mess, so he'll learn how to do for himself.

There are practical things he can do and if he's more in the background in this family he needs to be more hands on with parenting.

- Encourage brothers and sisters to play a part

- Involve extended family and friends

  If you're a single parent, especially if your children are young, you may need to get your extended family or friends involved. There is also the possibility of receiving funding for a cleaner directly through social services or through the Direct Payments system.

- Be specific in what you ask people to do

  You are much more likely to get a good response if you say, 'Can you hoover the living room?' rather than 'I need help with the hovering.'

- Be organised

  Most people who know me will laugh when they read this because I truly am one of the most disorganised people alive. However, even I have learnt the value of putting things in the same place so I don't lose them, keeping children's routines going no matter what and keeping on top of things so they don't overwhelm you. Another skill I've learnt is to finish the job I've started. There are always times when I have to drop everything because something dangerous is about to happen, but equally there are also times when my children can wait and I can finish what I'm doing.

Planning

A really important way of discovering and holding on to hope is to have a plan. It involves the ability to:

- step back and look at how the whole family is doing as well as the child with special needs;

- look back on things that have been really difficult and look at ways of avoiding it happening again; and

- think about the future and plan ahead.

(In the 'Moving on' section we will be looking more closely at planning.)

Moving on

Ways of being

I live in East London so I'm well aware of the barriers to hope. To get what we need for our children and ourselves will be a real battle. There are all the statutory agencies to deal with: the LEA, social services, housing, the health authority to name but a few. There are issues concerned with getting the right benefits and childcare. Then there is dealing with the local community so that our children are not discriminated against. The list is endless and if I were to tell you how to deal with all of them, this book would go on forever. What I can do is give you some ideas of skills to develop that will help you overcome the barriers to hope.

Knowing your rights and knowing where to go

The fact is few parents are told of their rights as parents of a child with a disability; if you don't build up knowledge yourself, it's unlikely that anyone else will do it for you. Chapter 2 'Building up support' and the Resource directory are good places to start. There are many organisations that can give you much more specialist help than me, with excellent publications and good courses to attend. There will be local community agencies that will be very helpful. But you have to go out and find them and you need to prepare yourself for disappointment and a lot of hard work.

Developing a good communication style

Once you have the information and the knowledge you then need to communicate in a way that gets you what you want without causing too many people offence along the way. I'm indebted here to a book called *Nonviolent Communication* by Marshall B. Rosenberg (1999). The idea behind the book is that many people face very trying conditions, so how can they gain language and communication skills that help them to remain strong but also still compassionate? Rosenberg is among many commentators who feel that we get into two styles of relating to others – passive or aggressive – neither of which is very helpful.

Passive

Inside – When we communicate like this inside we feel as though other people's feelings are our fault, as if we are in some way responsible for everyone's problems. Often, we also feel that it's our job to keep the peace and make sure everybody stays happy.

Outside – So if we feel like this inside how does it show itself outside when a professional is discussing our child?

- We are respectful in the way we speak to others but we have little or no confidence.

- If there is any tension in a conversation, we will immediately agree with the professional because we want at all costs to avoid the conflict. However, sometimes making a decision involves a bit of conflict and by agreeing we give up our right to be part of making that decision about our own child.

- We get into patterns of allowing others to do what they want and not what we think is best.

- We never really say what we really mean we're too busy being nice.

The outcome – At best we hope and wait for services for our child.

Aggressive

Inside – Sometimes as a response to being passive we become aware that for years we have been taking responsibility for other people's feelings without thinking about our own. It causes us to feel very angry. We start to express what we want but in a defensive and aggressive way because deep down we still feel afraid of giving our opinions and saying what we want and we feel guilty about having to do so.

Outside – How does it show itself in conversations with professionals about our child?

- We stand up for what they want but don't think for one minute about how the person we're speaking to might be feeling.

- We are not respectful in the way we speak to the other person and we can come across as hostile.

- We feel it's OK to attack the other person because the only thing that matters is what we want and think.

The outcome – Sometimes we get what we want in the short term, but in the long term we often face more barriers because we lose the goodwill of the professional who is working with our child. Therefore our child loses out.

There is, commentators say, a third way, a way of holding on to what you want and believe and at the same time taking other people into consideration and being respectful. Most commentators call this way being assertive.

Assertive

So when we're discussing our child with a professional:

Inside – We feel fine about what we say and do and we're not frightened to say things because it might offend somebody. We don't feel responsible for other people's feelings. And yet we also become aware that we can never get what we want at the expense of others' feelings. Which means that we are much more able to react to others out of compassion and we're much more willing to listen to their side of the story.

Outside – We express our point of view strongly and clearly but considerately.

- We talk with respect and confidence and do not put the other person down.

- We have a debate and try and solve the problems and issues without attacking the person.

- We finish the conversation with no build up of anger or fear.

The outcome – Not only are we more likely to come to an agreement but we will also be developing a good long-term relationship with the professional who is working with our child.

Finding our way around the system

In Chapter 1 'Beginnings', I described the services and professionals we meet as a maze. You need to learn to work your way around what's available for your family and your child. Some points to remember are:

- Don't try and do everything at once, stay focused, have a plan – know what you want and how you're going to get it.

- When you speak to professionals, be that on the phone, at an appointment, in a meeting or even informally, it is really important to take notes and date every conversation. Keep these notes in a file just in case you need to refer to them in the future.

- When you phone people don't expect them to call back! Be persistent – call every three days. When you get to speak to someone, continue to be persistent, firm and assertive, don't be fobbed off.

- If you're still not satisfied take it further – go higher, if needs be take legal advice or contact an advocacy group to represent you. Unfortunately sometimes this is a necessary action.

Strategies for the future

Circles of support

Circles of support are an idea I've come across since researching for the book (Falvey *et al.* 1997). I've had no direct experience of using one but I'm very excited about the possibility for my own family. For more information contact the Inclusion movement for details (see Parents for Inclusion and the Centre for Studies on Inclusive Education in the Resource directory).

Circles of support began when professionals in Canada working with adults who had severe physical and intellectual impairments were considering how best to support them to build relationships within their communities. Now they have been shown to work really well with a number of different groups of people including families.

What is the idea?

Circles of support try to find the best way to respect and support the child with a disability and his family's capability and interests. It looks at how this child could grow, develop and enrich others, not what he can't do. It looks at how this family can best develop in order to live a good and fulfilling life. They are not therefore support groups that sit around and bemoan how awful life is for this family. Rather they are a group of people who are committed to this family and this child. The circle of support is planned to be an ongoing group that meets regularly over a long period. It is based on the belief that we all have something to give to each other, that there will be mutual support within this group. In other words, interdependence.

Circles of support work in two key ways:

1 Listening to the family

   ■ Discovering how life is for the family

   ■ Getting to know them

   ■ Discovering particularly the interests and skills of the focus person/people, which may be the child or the parents.

2 Dreaming with the family

   ■ Helping to start thinking about the sort of hoped for life they want especially for the child with a disability

   ■ Helping them work out what the barriers are to this hopeful future

   ■ Doing the work that makes things happen: working through conflicts, doing creative problem solving, working out what to do next.

How does it work?

A circle of support is a group and all groups work best through two elements:

■ Making relationships – The family is placed in a varied group of listening people.

■ Being actively involved – Everyone should have the chance to participate.

It also needs some other things to really get things going:

■ Everybody needs to be committed to see positive change happen.

■ Parents need to start to see themselves and their child with special needs in the light of their gifts and capabilities.

■ The family need to believe that a different life is possible.

It takes time and the group needs to be willing to meet on a regular basis.

Why would it be useful for my family?

This theme of building a circle of support has been running through the book. All children benefit from being in a community that is larger than their nuclear family. For children with special needs the need for a wider community is greater as I don't believe there are enough resources within their parents no matter how amazing those parents are. For some, the old style extended family, with aunts and cousins on all the streets close by, works really well. However, for many of us there is no extended family nearby so a circle of support is something in its place.

A circle of support can be anyone: friends, family that are available, other parents with children with special needs, people who work with your child or workers who support you. There are particular ways that a circle of support can help families like ours:

■ It can help you feel loved and cared for.

■ It can help get rid of isolation by providing a network of mutual communication and support.

■ It is designed to be a place where problems can be solved and creative solutions found. In our family we need something like that everyday – Jono won't wear his shoes, Jono won't take his medication etc.

■ It can help stop the feeling of being overwhelmed by giving you another perspective.

■ It gives you hope.

When and how could I start?

To start a circle of support take the following steps as suggested by O'Brien on O'Brien (1998).

1   Work out who the circle is for – is the focus going to be you or your child? There is nothing wrong with you being the focus; the issue is that the focus must not be confused.

2   Start thinking about the members of your group.

Whoever you chose they need to be people who:

■ you can trust;

■ you know will be prepared to be committed for a good length of time;

■ are more likely to listen and be thoughtful rather than jump in straight away with advice; and

■ are open to the idea of positive change.

The group needs someone who can manage and lead a group well, who is good at involving people and good at listening. People like this can be found in different places; it may be a friend, one of your children's teachers, a family worker, or your social worker. Ideally it should be someone who has good links in the local community. As well as that it's also good to have:

■ at least one other parent who also has a child with a disability;

■ someone who's good at practical problem solving and creative thinking;

■ someone who's good at making things happen in the community;

■ at least one person from a statutory service like social services or a voluntary organisation like Barnardos or Mencap.

3   If your response to the previous point is, 'I don't know anyone!' start talking about it to everyone you know – at school, at work, in your support group, with your family and friends. Tell your child's school, social worker and any other workers who support your family about the idea. It's amazing how many people you'll find who want to get involved.

4   Once you've found someone who is willing to lead the group get them to help you choose and invite the other people. For a group like this you need to be thinking of between seven and ten people.

5   Start when you're ready by sending invitations out for the first group meeting. It's good to eat together, but start as you mean to go on by asking them to bring a contribution of food and drink with them!

MAPs

This is a tool, a way of working, which breaks down the barriers to hope. It was developed by the same Canadian professionals (Falvey *et al.* 1997) and is something that can be done in a circle of support or in a variety of other groups.

We've used this at Exchange and people came out with some amazing things. As a group it's really moved us on. It's a way of looking at the future in a hopeful way and bringing a group of people together. The example I'm using here is the way it could be used in a circle of support. A MAP has the following features:

- The big question it is asking is 'What kind of future do you want?'

- This process is like a proper map, with a starting point, a destination and a possible route to stop you getting lost.

- The process itself is a series of questions:
  - What is the history of the person who is the focus of the group?
  - What is your dream? (Where do you want to get to – what is your destination?)
  - What is your nightmare? (What do you live in fear of happening? How can you avoid it?)
  - Who are you? (one-word descriptions – think of ways to describe the person, such as the relationships he has, his strengths, the choices he makes, the places he goes)
  - What does the person need now?
  - How shall we plan to build on the strengths he has, avoid the dangers and answer his needs?

Afterthought

On any day, in any week of the life of a parent of a child with a disability, the most important thing is hope. It's the hardest thing to find and the most difficult thing to hold on to and yet I believe it's essential for living. The idea of this chapter is to make that process a little easier. After all, we and our children deserve it.

End thoughts

If this book has done anything, I hope it has begun a process of rethinking and looking again.

Look again at our children

> ☞ **Si's story**
>
> Jono has given so much back, and continues to challenge my preconceptions, my ideals and my way of living. As a person he has had so much influence on me for the good that one smile or cuddle can undo all the pent up rage about destroyed furniture, a chaotic house or no sleep.

Our children have much to give: they have gifts, contributions and important things to say to us, our family, friends and the wider community. We all desperately need them.

Look again at us

Our children have taken us on a journey. Many parents I've spoken to have commented how they are different people now. They talk of being stronger, more tolerant, more assertive and confident. I see many changes in myself too. It is time we looked more closely at who we are. Every day, every sleepless night we already do things that most of the rest of society wouldn't have a clue about. Do we not deserve a good and fulfilling life? Do our children not deserve to realise their full potential?

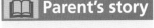 **Parent's story**

I appreciate life more.

The choices are ours – this is not the life we planned but it does not have to be the end. The future, though undoubtedly challenging, will be exciting, and could well offer far more than we ever imagined or expected – the possibilities are endless!

Resource directory

General organisations

ADD/ADHD Family Support Group
1a High Street
Dilton Marsh
Westbury BA13 4DL
Tel: 01373 826045
National support group run by parents for parents. Provides a good telephone helpline and really good down to earth support and advice.

AFASIC
2nd floor, 50–52 Great Sutton Street
London EC1V 0
Tel: 020 7490 9410
Helpline: 0845 355 5577 (Mon–Fri 11 a.m.–2 p.m.)
www.afasic.org.uk
Parent-led organisation which helps children and young people with speech and language impairments. Provides information and advice on all aspects of life from accessing speech therapy to benefits. Has 34 local groups and Regional Development Officers.

Asian People with Disabilities Alliance (APDA)
Disability Alliance Centre
Old Rectory
Central Middlesex Hospital
Acton Lane
Park Royal
London NW10 7NS
Tel: 020 8961 6773

Association for Spina Bifida and Hydrocephalus
42 Park Road
Peterborough PE1 2UQ
Tel: 01733 555988 (9 a.m.–5 p.m.)
www.asbah.org
Provides advice and practical support, a network of professional advisers and has expertise in advocating for education for children. Website has extensive information and links to local associations.

British Epilepsy Association
New Anstey House
Gate Way Drive
Yeadon
Leeds LS19 7XY
Tel: 0113 210 8800
Helpline: 0808 800 5050
www.epilepsy.org.uk
Largest member-led organisation in UK, provides telephone and email helpline, local branches and support groups. Has an accredited volunteer scheme that provides home support to families and individuals. Good website with lots of information.

Brittle Bone Society
30 Guthrie Street
Dundee DD1 5BS
Tel: 01382 204 446
Helpline: 0800 028 2459
www.brittlebone.org
Offers: Local support groups and regular news-letter, advice on funds and grants for specialist equipment, specialist occupational therapists who visit families in their homes, help with some financial needs and short-term loan of equipment.

Care Co-ordination Network UK
Social Policy Research Unit
University of York
Heslington
York YO10 5DD
Tel: 01904 433605
www.york.ac.uk/inst/spru/ccnuk.htm
Organisation set up to share information
and promote good practice about co-ordi-
nating support for families with children
with special needs in the UK.

Carers UK
Ruth Pitter House
20–25 Glasshouse Yard
London EC1A 4JT
Tel: 020 7490 8818
Carers Line: 0808 808 7777
www.carersonline.org.uk
Provides information and advice about all
aspects of being a carer from health to
juggling work. Extensive website gives
details of all registered carers associations
in the UK.

**Carers National Association Northern
Ireland**
58 Howard St
Belfast BT1 6PJ
Tel: 028 9043 9843

Carers Scotland
33 Leven Drive
Hurlsford
Kilmarnock KA1 5HH
Tel: 01563 525822

Carers Wales
River House
Ynys Bridge Court
Gwaelod y Garth
Cardiff CF15 9SS
Tel: 029 2081 1370

Children's Heart Federation
52 Kennington Oval
London SE11 5SW
Tel: 020 7820 8517
Helpline: 0808 808 5000 (Mon–Fri 9.30
a.m.–9.30 p.m.)
www.childrens-heart-fed.org.uk

Offers: range of support groups for families ofchildren with heart conditions,
national helpline, conferences, special
holidays and events forfamilies, education for teachers and lots of information
from different heart conditions to looking after your children's teeth. Very easy
to access website.

CLIMB
The Quadrangle
Crewe Hall
Weston Rd
Crewe CW1 6UR
Tel: 0870 770 0325
Helpline: 0870 770 0326
www.climb.org.uk
National information and advice centre
for children, young people and families
affected by a metabolic disease. Offers:
information, support and advice by tele-
phone helpline and post, signposting to
other organisations, national network of
groups and trained volunteer befrienders.
Some financial assistance available.

Contact a Family
209–211 City Rd
London EC1V 1JN
Tel: 020 7608 8700
Helpline: 0808 808 3555 (Mon–Fri 10
a.m.–4 p.m.)
www.cafamily.org.uk
National charity providing support, information and advice for families with
disabled children. Very good on rare disorders. Has a network of personal contacts
and helps develop local and national support groups. Excellent informative website.

Contact a Family Northern Ireland
Bridge Community Centre
50 Railway St
Lisburn BT28 1XP
Tel: 028 9262 7552

Contact a Family Scotland
Norton Park
57 Albion Rd
Edinburgh EH7 5QY
See Contact a Family for helpline and
website.

Contact a Family Wales
Trident Court
East Moors Rd
Cardiff CF24 5TD
Tel: 029 2044 9569
See Contact a Family for helpline and
website.

Continence Foundation
307 Hatton Square
16 Baldwin's Gardens
London EC1N 7RJ
Tel: 020 7404 6875
www.continence-foundation.org .uk
Website provides information about to
get hold of specialist equipment and
products to help with incontinence.

Council for Disabled Children
8 Wakley St
London ECIV 7QE
Tel: 020 7843 6000
www.ncb.org.uk

Cystic Fibrosis Trust
11 London Rd
Bromley
Kent BR1 1BY
Tel: 020 8464 7211
Helpline: 0845 859 1000
www.cftrust.org.uk

Disability Now
6 Market Rd
London N7 9PW
Tel: 020 7619 7317
www.disabilitynow.org.uk
Award winning newspaper for everyone
with an interest in disability.

Disability Rights Commission
DRC Helpline
Freepost
MID O2164
Stratford-upon-Avon CV37 9BR
Tel: 0845 762 2633
Helpline: 0845 762 2633
www.drc-gb.org
Independent body established by law to
get rid of discrimination.

Down's Syndrome Association
155 Mitcham Rd
London SW17 9PG
Tel: 020 8682 4001
www.downs-syndrome.org.uk

Dyspraxia Foundation
8 West Alley
Hitchin
Herts SG5 1EG
Tel: 01462 454996
Helpline: 01462 454986
www.dyspraxiafoundation.org.uk

Homes Fit for Children Campaign
c/o HODIS
17 Priory St
York YO1 6ET
www.hffc.org.uk

Homestart UK
2 Salisbury Rd
Leicester LE1 7QR
Tel: 0116 233 9953
Helpline: 08000 686368
www.home-start.org.uk

Jessica Kingsley Publishers
116 Pentonville Rd
London N1 9JB
Tel: 020 7833 2307
www.jkp.com
Excellent publisher for special needs
resources.

Mencap
123 Golden Lane
London EC1Y 0RT
Tel: 020 7454 0454
Helpline: 020 7696 5593
www.mencap.org.uk

Muscular Dystrophy Campaign
Nattrass House
7–11 Prescott Place
London SW4 6BS
Tel: 020 7720 8055
www.muscular-dystrophy.org

National Autistic Society
393 City Rd
London EC1V 1NG
Tel: 020 7833 2299
Helpline: 0870 600 8585
www.nas.org.uk

National Council for One Parent Families
255 Kentish Town Rd
London NW5 2LX
Tel: 020 7428 5400
Helpline: 0800 018 5026
www.oneparentfamilies.org.uk

National Deaf Children's Society
15 Dufferin St
London EC1Y 8UR
Tel: 020 7250 0123
Freephone: 0808 800 8880
www.ndcs.org.uk

Parents with Attitude
PO Box 1727
Sheffield S11 8WS
www.parentswithattitude.fsnet.co.uk

Royal National Institute of the Blind (RNIB)
105 Judd St
London WC1H 9NE
Tel: 020 7388 1266
Helpline: 0845 766 9999
www.rnib.org.uk

Scope
6 Market Rd
London N7 9PW
Tel: 020 7619 7100
Helpline: 0808 800 3333
www.scope.org.uk

Sense (National Deaf–blind and Rubella Association)
11–13 Clifton Terrace
Finsbury Park
London N4 3SR
Tel: 020 7272 7774
www.sense.org.uk

Sickle Cell Society
54 Station Rd
Harlesdon
London NW10 4UA
Tel: 020 8961 7795
www.sicklecellsociety.org

SWAN (Syndromes without a name)
6 Acorn Close
Great Wyrley
Walsall WS6 6HP
Tel: 01922 701234
undiagnosed@clara.co.uk
Provide a newsletter and information.

Young Minds
102–108 Clerkenwell Rd
London EC1M 5AX
Tel: 020 7336 8445
Parents' Information Service:
Freephone: 0800 018 2138
www.youngminds.org.uk

Education

Advisory Centre for Education (ACE)
1c Aberdeen Studios
22 Highbury Grove
London N5 2DQ
Tel: 020 7354 8321
Freephone: 0808 800 5793
www.ace-ed.org.uk
Offers free guidance and advice on all aspects of state education. Has a comprehensive guide on special education as well as a number of other publications.

Centre for Studies on Inclusive Education (CSIE)
Room 25203, S Block
Frenchay Campus
Cold Harbour Lane
Bristol BS16 1QU
Tel: 0117 344 4007
www.inclusion.org.uk
Independent organisation working towards the inclusion of all pupils with disabilities and learning difficulties into ordinary schools. Gives information and advice to parents about inclusive education.

Department for Education and Skills (DfES)
Special Education Needs Division
Mowden Hall GF Area E
Staindrop Rd
Darlington DL3 9BG
Tel: 01325 391 223
www.dfes.gov.uk
Provides guidance on education and has a range of useful information, as well as a parents' section on their website.

Department of Education Northern Ireland
Rathgel House
Balloo Rd
Bangor BT19 7PR
Tel: 028 9127 9279
www.deni.gov.uk

Education Otherwise
PO Box 7420
London N9 9SG
Tel: 0870 730 0074
www.education-otherwise.org
Provides support and information for families whose children are being educated outside school.

Inclusion Press
24 Thorne Crescent,
Toronto
Ontario
Canada H6H 285

Independent Panel for Special Education Advice (IPSEA)
6 Carlow Mews
Woodbridge
Suffolk IP12 1EA
Tel: 01394 382814
Freephone: 0800 018 4016
www.ipsea.org.uk
Has independent experts who give advice to parents who disagree with their LEA's views of their child's educational needs. They can represent you at tribunals. However, they are often over-subscribed and there is a waiting list for this service.

Independent Special Education Advice (ISEA)
164 High St
Dalkeith EH22 1AY
Tel: 0131 454 0096
Helpline: 0131 454 0082

Parents for Inclusion
Unit 2
70 South Lambeth Rd
London SW8 1RL
Tel: 020 7735 7735
Helpline: 020 7582 5008 (Tues, Wed and Thurs 10–12 a.m. and 1–3 p.m.) 0800 652 3145
www.parentsforinclusion.org
National charity run by par-ents for parents. Provides: helpline, excellent training for professionals and parents, help in setting up inclusion groups in schools and linking parents with other organi-sations in the Inclusion Now network.

SNAP Cymru (Special Needs Advisory Project – education)
10 Coopers Yard
Curran Rd
Cardiff CF10 5NB
Tel: 029 2038 8776
www.snapcymru.org

Benefits and other sources of help

Benefit Enquiry Line for People with Disabilities
9th Floor
Victoria House
Ormskirk Rd
Preston PR1 2QP
Freephone: 0800 882200
www.dwp.gov.uk

Benefit Enquiry Line for Disabled People
Northern Ireland
Freephone: 0800 2206

Disability Alliance
Universal House
88–94 Wentworth Street
London E1 7SA
Tel: 020 7247 8776
Rights advice line: 020 7247 8763 (Mon and Wed 2–4 p.m.)
www.disabilityalliance.org
Leading authority on social security benefitsfor disabled people. Aim to break the link between disability and poverty through information, advice and campaigning for change. Publish a number of publications including the *Disability Rights Handbook* (updated each year).

Family Fund Trust
PO Box 50
York YO1 9ZX
Tel: 01904 621115
www.familyfundtrust.org.uk
Fund will give lump sums for specific items for families who have a severely disabled child. Your social and economic situation is taken into account. They will consider any request for whatever you need most. They have an excellent website with a whole range of information.

Family Welfare Association
The Grants Officer
501–505 Kingsland Rd
London E8 4AU
Tel: 020 7254 6251
This organisation administers a variety of grants although they can't help with anything already provided by statutory authorities. Applications must be made through your social worker.

Motability
Goodman House
Station Approach
Harlow, Essex CM20 2ET
Tel: 01279 635666
www.motability.co.uk
They will help people who get the higher rate of the mobility component of DLA to obtain cars.

Adaptations and equipment

Abilitynet
PO Box 94
Warwick CV34 5WS
Tel: 01926 312847
Helpline: 0800 269545
www.Abilitynet.org.uk
Advice and information on computers and disability. Offers assessments for individuals(children and adults) and extensive links to suppliers of adaptive computer equipment and software.

Crelling Harnesses for Disabled Ltd
12 Crescent East
Thornton Cleveleys
Lancs FY5 3LJ
Tel: 01253 852298
www.crelling.com
Excellent company who can supply harnesses and seatbelts for most types of impairments. Also supply steel safety buckles for escape artists and walking reins that look 'cool' for older children.

Disabled Living Centres Council
Redbank House
4 St Chad's St
Manchester M8 8QA
Tel: 0161 834 1044
www.dlcc.org.uk

Disabled Living Foundation
380–384 Harrow Rd
London W9 2HU
Tel: 020 7289 6111
Helpline: 0845 130 9177
www.dlf.org.uk
Provides information on technology and
equipment, a demonstration centre
where you can book an appointment
with a trained adviser and a database of
second-hand equipment. Website has
factsheets and online shopping.

Muscular Dystrophy Campaign
Nattrass House
7–11 Prescott Place
London SW4 6BS
Tel: 020 7720 8055
www.muscular-dystrophy.org
This organisation can help families with
other conditions as well as neuromuscu-
lar conditions. They have published the
Adaptions Manual, a very helpful publication.

**RADAR (Royal Association for
Disability and Rehabilitation)**
12 City Forum
250 City Rd
London EC1V 8AF
Tel: 020 7250 3222
www.radar.org.uk
Have a number of helpful guides such as
the guide to Disabled Facilities Grants
(they can also advise if you have difficulties). They also publish *Door to Door* about
help with transport and a holiday guide.

REMAP
Hazeldene
Ightham
Kent TN15 9AD
Tel: 01732 883818
Helpline: 0845 130 0456
www.remap.org.uk

Organisation of engineers with 100 local
panels in the UK. They can design and
make equipment in consultation with
doctors and occupational therapists.

Fun, leisure and holidays

Action for Leisure
c/o Warwickshire College
Moreton Morrell Centre
Moreton Morrell
Warwick CV35 9BL
Tel: 01926 650 195
www.actionforleisure.org.uk
Information and advice about how to
access play and leisure for disabled children, young people and adults, offers a
mail order service for a range of great
inexpensive play and leisure items and
advice on specialist suppliers.

Family Holiday Association
16 Mortimer St
London W1T 3JL
Tel: 020 7436 3304
www.fhaonline.org.uk
Provides grants for families in real need
of a break for one week's holiday of their
choice. The family must be referred by
social services, a health professional or
local voluntary organisations.

Formative Fun
Education House
Horn Park Business Centre
Broadwindsor Rd
Beaminster
Dorset DT8 3PT
Tel: 01308 868999
www.formativefun.com
Really good games and toy supplier for
children with learning difficulties. Takes a
number of conditions then looks at par-
ticular toys and games that would suit a
child with that condition. Has shops,
mail order and online shopping.

The Happy Puzzle Company Ltd
PO Box 24041
London NW4 2ZN
Tel: 0800 376 3725
www.happypuzzle.co.uk
Supplier of puzzles, games and teasers. Some are very useful for children with dyslexia and dyspraxia. Has special needs advisers available to speak over the phone. Mail order and online shopping also available.

HELP (Holiday Endeavour for Lone Parents)
57 Owston Rd
Carcroft
Doncaster DN6 8DA
Tel: 01302 728 791
Provides low cost holidays for any lone parent and their children. Families with children with disabilities may be sponsored.

Holiday Care
2nd Floor
Imperial Buildings
Victoria Road
Horley RH6 7PZ
Tel: 01293 774535
www.holidaycare.org.uk
Provides information about all types of holiday for people with special needs including family holidays. They can also help with reservations.

Kidsactive (HAPA)
Prior's Rd
Bishop's Park
London SW6 3LA
Tel: 020 7731 1435
www.kidsactive.org.uk
An organisation that promotes play for children with disbilities. They run six adventure playgrounds. They provide information and training to parents.

Write Away
1 Thorpe Close
London W10 5XL
Tel: 020 8964 4225
Provide a penfriend club for children with disabilities.

Therapies and treatments

Association of Professional Music Therapists (APMT)
24 Hamlyn Rd
Glastonbury
Somerset BA6 8HT
Tel: 01458 834919
www.apmt.org

Autism Research Unit
School of Health Sciences
University of Sunderland
Sunderland SR2 7EE
Tel: 0191 567 0420
www.osiris.sunderland.ac.uk/autism/index.html
Excellent research on gluten- and casein-free diet with good links to other sites.

British Association of Art Therapists
Mary Ward House
5 Tavistock House
London WC1N 9SN
Tel: 020 7383 3774
www.baat.org.uk

Hanen UK
6 Dungoyne St
Maryhill
Glasgow G20 0BA
Tel: 0141 9465433
www.hanen.org
Early intervention therapy for children with speech and language disorders. Among other resources Hanen has produced two parent guides for use with children of all abilities: *It Takes Two*.

Makaton Vocabulary Development Project
31 Firwood Drive
Camberley
Surrey GU15 3QD
Tel: 01276 61390
www.makaton.org

Pyramid Educational Consultants Ltd
17 Prince Albert St
Brighton
East Sussex BN1 3HF
Tel: 01273 728888
www.pecs-uk.com
Provides training, information and resources to set up the PECs (Picture Exchange Communication System) for children with speech and communication difficulties.

The Options Institute and Fellowship
2080 S Undermountain Rd
Sheffield
MA 01257
USA
Tel: 413 229 2100

Group work manual

Introduction

The session outlines presented in this section are set out as a ten-week course but it could easily be used as ongoing material within a support group. Each session has handouts, however you may find sections of the book helpful as well especially the parents' stories and these can be photocopied.

The framework of the course is based on the following ten principles for facilitators.

1 Empathy and listening principle

There is an overwhelming need for parents of children with special needs to tell their story. Many live with chronic stress in often traumatic circumstances. Often they are not used to people really listening to them. A common experience is that their story is too much for others. So what happens instead is that people will try and offer advice and solutions as a way of fixing their lives. In the book I listed the sort of listeners parents need. People who:

- will hear their story and connect with them;
- can handle their pain and stress;
- don't jump in with lots of advice and many words;
- are there for us and who are not just drawing the attention back to themselves.

Built into the structure of the course, as an integral part, is *storytelling and listening*. To encourage parents listening to each other means that facilitators need to model good listening. That means allowing people to stay with their pain and difficulty and not rushing on too quickly to offer solutions. It means challenging within yourself the reaction that their raw emotion might have on you – be that anger, anxiety or despair. It means reflecting back and summarising what they're saying in such a way that it encourages them to say more. And, it means remembering that what they say first of all may just be the tip of an iceberg. If you can stay with empathy, it gives them time to get in touch with other related but more powerful feelings. Doing so is such a gift to them because it will help them really understand what is going on. Ultimately, that is often the driving force that enables parents to reframe their view of themselves and their children. In other words, it is what helps them to move on.

Much can be achieved through listening well but it is hard and delicate work that takes strength and skill. You're not just listening for people's words but for their feelings. And as a group facilitator you're seeking to do this for everyone. That's why I believe it is really important in groups like these to have a co-facilitator.

2 Acceptance principle

Closely linked to listening is acceptance. It's incredibly important that you do not rush to judge any parent. It's useful to ask yourself why you're judging them and very often it has the same root as offering advice. You want to put a barrier up between them and you because what they're telling you is overwhelming and frightening. They might be very angry and that anger could be directed at you. They might be very chaotic and disturbing the group. Making a quick judgement about someone distances us from him or her. It protects us but it does not help them to move on. It is not your job to diagnose or to offer prescriptive advice. Instead go in with a fluid, open and receptive state of mind. Respect the uniqueness and complexity of each parent; we all have the capacity of being incredibly strong and vulnerable at the same time. Parents of children with special needs are just under more pressure than the average person so show their vulnerability more.

3 Relationship principle

Many parents who will come on a course or attend support groups have lost relationships; they feel disconnected from people. A key part of facilitation is to help and enable them to re-establish relationships. Helping people to connect with each other through noticing what they have in common starts this process. There is a huge sense of relief when people start to realise they are 'not the only one'. Also often parents come when they are at the end of their tether with their child. They may feel they have lost or are in danger of losing their relationship with their child. A key principle behind the book and course material is discovering or rediscovering the enjoyment and satisfaction of the parent–child relationship.

Finally, parents will often be very isolated within their communities. The course material encourages parents to make networks within their locality. Part of the job of the facilitator is encouraging parents to find ways for them and their family to be included in the fullest sense in their own community.

4 Empowerment principle

In any group, facilitators can easily take on the role of expert. In fact many parents of children with special needs will be expecting you to play that role. After all, many of the people they have come into contact with so far have claimed to be an expert on their child. Although as facilitator you need to be a leader and a guide, your job is in fact to help parents find their own expertise. They come in demoralised and weary; they have lost trust in their own ability to make judgements and decisions. So, part of your role as facilitator is to help parents discover and find their own strengths and make their own conclusions and choices. What are the implications of this?

Not feeling the need to be in control all the time

Groups can be chaotic places and it's important not to be afraid of that chaos. There are good ways of intervening that maintain the structure of the group without taking over.

Help parents do things for themselves

You can support people and help them plan and think through issues. However, the best way people start to feel powerful again is to reach their own decisions and take their own actions.

Learn flexibility

Sometimes things don't go to plan and that's to be expected. Often discussions take longer than the time you've given them. What you need to work out as the group is progressing is what of the material that's been planned are key issues that must be covered and what can be done at a later date. It's called thinking on your feet.

Avoid the temptation of advising

Often parents will ask you directly for advice. It could be that you have the information they want. However, a good way of dealing with this is to open the question up to the group. Often group members will have at least part if not all of the answer. Only then, should you give the information. That way other parents will feel empowered and you will simply be part of the process of sharing.

5 Value and encouragement principle

If ever there was a group of people who need their self-esteem to be built up and who need to feel valued, it is parents with children with special needs. Their ability to feel good about themselves has been badly damaged by their experience. Most parents, especially in the early years, are working from a position of guilt – 'This must be something I've done wrong,' – they have a very low opinion of their own parenting. So often they need your observations of events they manage but take for granted: 'You were up all night with her and you still managed to get them all to school on time –

now, I think that's really impressive.' Also, many parents of children with special needs very quickly become carers rather than people. They stop seeing looking after themselves as at all important, it is at best very low down their list of priorities. Another key focus of the book and course material is to change that view. It is to start to see looking after themselves as a vital step in the moving on process.

6 Problem-solving principle

At the beginning, particularly, parents want help finding solutions to immediate problems. This is often a real crisis where there is no time to reflect. So they need facilitators who can think clearly and creatively and help them find their own problem-solving skills. They also need access to information such as how to get free nappies and how to apply for DLA.

7 Respect principle

Any facilitator needs to remember to be respectful with people's lives. However, parents of children with disabilities really do need to be treated with dignity. It is important to honour the trauma and struggle they have gone through. It's vital that you don't patronise them.

Part of respect is to be aware of how powerful groups can be – positively and negatively. A fundamental principle of group work is to do no harm. It's better to be nervous and humble about your abilities than create 'irreparable damage' with families' lives. There is a time and place to take risks but you need to be cautious.

8 Knowledge and self-knowledge principle

Facilitators need to have access to a wide information base, however, the most important knowledge is what is going on internally for yourself. You need to know your strengths, your limits, your prejudices and your preferences. You are seeking to facilitate change in people's views of themselves, their children and what is possible in their lives. You need to be able to think creatively and laterally. Your judgements, interpretations and preferences could block that process.

You need to be aware that you are always learning, that means regularly reviewing what you're doing to see what changes need to be made. You will learn every time you run a group or deliver a course.

Finally, it's important to know what it's like to be a participant in a group; to experience feeling challenged and vulnerable. If at all possible have the experience of being in a group before facilitating.

9 Support principle

Groups and courses for parents with children with special needs are best facilitated through team work. One of the main themes in the book and course material is building up support systems for parents. It's vital that facilitators do this for themselves. A lone isolated worker, no matter how good a facilitator, will not be able to deliver the same level of support to parents as a facilitator or co-facilitator with a network of support behind them. Also if you are asking parents to build up their support shouldn't you also do it for yourself? Creating a network and finding a co-facilitator may take time but in the long run it will be time well spent.

Co-facilitator

It maybe that your co-leader takes an equal share in leading and presenting to the group or, that you take the main responsibility for leading and he or she has other roles such as making sure everyone is included, checking group dynamics and summarising. This is likely to depend on personality, preference and experience. However, when the group is finished it's a tremendous help to have someone to work with to de-brief the group, plan and discuss problematic issues (and sometimes people!).

Supervision

Therapeutic supervision for facilitating any support group is general good practice. For this type of group and course I would say it was critical. It is very likely that at some stage in the group process parents in this position will disclose intense and raw emotions. If there is unresolved trauma in their lives, perhaps from childhood or adolescence, it is quite possible that the stress of parenting a child with a disability will draw this to the surface. You need to be prepared that this is likely to affect you at times and trigger issues from your own life. If it's difficult to get hold of a supervisor, consider the idea of having group supervision with colleagues doing similar work and getting someone to facilitate this group.

Network of community support

I really think it's important that a support group or course of this nature is not run in isolation. Very early on in the group you are likely to have parents who need help that you cannot give or who are asking questions that you have no answer to, be that concerning housing, social services or educational issues. You need to know who to refer to and seek information from. This works better if you've spent some time building up a relationship with, for example, the local speech and language service. It's also good if professionals in the community know what you're doing.

10 Commitment principle

Parents in this position are not going to be helped by a quick fix approach. It's much better if you are able and prepared to have a long-term relationship with them. Jack Pierpoint and Marsha Forest (1998: 97) put it very well: 'There are no magic wands. There is just the long haul, hard work that all of us must do to realise fully lived lives in these complex and challenging times.'

Parents need people who can go at their pace. Parents are often very tired if not exhausted. Sometimes they have no resources to process or to take on new information; they are simply surviving. Coming to terms with who your children are and how best to meet their need is a lifetime's journey with many side roads, cul-de-sacs and roundabouts.

Setting up a group or course

Practical points to consider before setting up a group or course are as follows.

Funding

If funding is a problem, there are many avenues to consider. As encouraging parent partnership has been such a central part of recent government legislation, it's worth approaching government initiatives, such as Sure Start, Children's Fund as well as local authorities. It's always a good idea to work in partnership with other agencies to gain funding. Working for example with voluntary agencies such as Mencap or Family Welfare Association may also be a way of recruiting parents.

Publicity and outreach

Think carefully about publicity, you don't want to put people off. A poster is a good idea with not too much detailed text but a bright attractive format. Put copies in all the public places, such as libraries and health centres. Make sure that the right contact details are on it, there's nothing worse than a parent phoning and only ever getting an answer-machine message.

What will always be better than publicity is a personal contact. If a parent has met you before they are much more likely to come. That's often easy to achieve in a school setting but sometimes may involve home visits. Even though these are time consuming they can really pay dividends.

Venue

The venue needs to be local to where parents are, easy to get to and preferably somewhere they are used to going to. It's better if it's a room rather than a hall, where parents are not going to be disturbed. You need to have a second room that can be used as a crèche, access to refreshments and somewhere where windows open and the heating works. Comfortable chairs really help, as does a flipchart and somewhere to display information.

Timing

Think carefully about timing, it's something that catches a lot of people out. In my experience of ten years of running groups for parents the best time to launch a new group or course is September, the worst time is the summer term. When you're planning courses you need to account for half terms and any odd days schools have off. Also it's not a good idea to run too close to Christmas (too much going on), equally bear in mind the time of Ramadan as Muslim parents are likely to be fasting and this will affect attendance. When you're thinking of times of day, you need to find out what time nurseries and schools finish so that parents have time to go and collect their children.

Refreshments and crèche

For parents of young children, a crèche may be a reason for attending the course. It's definitely a major attraction for a number of parents. Make sure you have regular contact with the people who run the crèche so if there are any problems they can be ironed out quickly.

Refreshments can also surprisingly be a draw. I can understand that, the chance to have an undisturbed cup of tea and a nice biscuit can be a real pleasure. Do small things well, good quality biscuits, a friendly, well set out room say a lot about how much you value people.

Course outline

Core components

The sessions of the course are structured around key components.

Off-load time

At the beginning of each session there will be an opportunity for group members to off load about the events in their week. This should be a limited time with the acknowledgement that if a major issue is disclosed there will be some time given to return to it. Be careful with this section, if you're not careful it can take up half of any session. It has to be facilitated sensitively and yet with good boundaries. Two good questions to ask are:

How do you feel about your week?

Is there any action that needs taking about what happened this week?

Storytelling and listening

Storytelling and listening are key ingredients to this course. Parents' stories will inform the way the course or group goes, far more than anything a facilitator says. They have important stories that need unpacking and careful listening. The key issue here is enabling parents to listen to each other. Each week the parents will work in pairs, both will tell their stories, both will listen. Each week as well as summarising the key points to listening you'll add a bit more about what true listening is. So that hopefully by the end they will all have experienced quality listening.

Something funny

When I thought about planning a course, I thought about how significant laughter had been to Exchange. How often, even at the worse points, people laugh. At the beginning of any group, laughter is a great way of establishing connections between group members.

Something to learn

This is the main facilitator presentation. In the early weeks it's very information based but as the course progresses it becomes more group exercises and small group work.

Feelings check

This course is holistic and crucial to the book and course is the concept that what is going on internally for the parent is critical to the present and future.

Practical action

This aims to combine what they've learned and how they feel into what they're going to do. This is not prescriptive and will not be the same for each parent. However, moving on at some point is about action. It helps to make a decision even if it takes a while to follow it through.

Looking after yourself

This is an element at the end of each session and it is designed to encourage group members to look after themselves in a variety of ways.

Facilitator notes

As well as core components, each course outline will have notes for the facilitator on a number of issues.

Setting the scene

This is to consider everything that needs to be thought of before a group starts. It covers practical information and information gathering particularly relevant to the theme of that chapter, as well as networking that may need to be done with other agencies beforehand.

Key points for facilitators

This section looks at:

- Material – the essential points to each session that should be covered even if others have to be dropped.
- Group dynamics – the different aspects of group dynamics that might occur at different stages of the course or development of the support group.

■ Follow up – the practical follow up needed may include information gathering for individual parents or actual referrals to appropriate agencies.

Course content

It's useful to prepare for the sessions by reading the relevant chapters within the book and using the Resource directory as back up. For extra reading, use the Bibliography section.

Session 1: Introduction

Session 2: Beginnings

Session 3: Building up support

Session 4: Communication and relationship building

Session 5: Behaviour

Session 6: Stress

Session 7: Facing the feelings

Session 8: Families

Session 9: Hope

Session 10: Facing the future

There are handout sheets for you to copy and distribute in the Appendix.

Session 1: Introduction

Facilitator notes

Setting the scene

- Preparations – Seating, refreshments, enrolment forms, folders for handouts, flipchart, pens, paper
- **Handout 1** Course content

  Handout 2 Listening

Key points for facilitators

Material

Ground rules

Here are a few suggested ground rules:

- Confidentiality except for child protection;
- Group members take responsibility for themselves – if you don't understand something, ask;
- Everyone has a right to disagree and defend their opinions but not to put people down or attack people;
- If you feel distressed about what's being talked about you should be able to take time out, but you should also be able to talk to a facilitator afterwards.

Connection

A lot of time this week will be spent on introductions. A lot of facilitation work should be going into helping people to find common ground with each other.

Information

People will be given a lot of information this week about the content of the course and how it runs. This needs to be balanced with space for their concerns, anxieties and expectations.

Listening

This is a key issue to learn this week. Give a clear explanation as to why it's so important and let the brainstorming ideas come from them, but let there be enough time to actually have a go at storytelling and listening.

Group dynamics

What happens in the first week is the very early stage of group dynamics, sometimes called the '**forming**' stage of a group.

Entering a group is a risky step for most people, it might mean:

- To expose themselves to strangers;
- To look at areas of their lives which they have being trying to avoid;
- To try out new ways of thinking and feeling; new belief systems;
- To try out new ways of behaving.

For parents of children with special needs those anxieties are increased by fear that their parenting will be attacked and also that they might breakdown within the group and reveal too much about themselves. At the beginning, a parent's ability to listen and take in what is being said is overshadowed by other worries and desires they might be having such as:

- Will people accept me?
- I really want to be close to others.
- I really want to be cared for and looked after.

This is not usually a time for much self-disclosure, in fact people revealing personal issues too early within a group can feel really exposed. At this stage the energy of the group is going into 'being there'.

Running order

- **Introduce facilitators**
- **Practical information**

    Time, toilets, crèche, refreshments

■ **Off-load time**

Facilitators introduce this by showing how it's done:

How I feel
Action I need to take.

■ **Ground rules**

■ **Introduce the group**

Pairs exercise – introduce yourselves and your children

■ **What do you want from the course?**

Large group exercise:

What are you expecting to get out of it?
What are your hopes?
What are your fears?

■ **Outline of course content**

Give out copies of **Handout 1** Course content.

■ **Comments and questions**

Opportunity for parents to ask any questions about the course

■ **The way the course works**

Off-load time
Storytelling and listening
Something funny
Something to learn
How things make me feel
Practical action
Looking after yourself

■ **Something to learn**

Listening – Emphasise the importance of telling your story and being listened to. In small groups ask the parents what the basics of good listening is. Feedback and flipchart the results. Give out copies of **Handout 2** Listening.

■ Storytelling and listening

Twenty-four hours in my life: split the group into pairs

This is about parents telling their own stories and needs to be handled sensitively. Some parents will want an opportunity to talk straight away; others will find this process intimidating and be very concerned about the facilitator's reaction. Parents should be allowed to do what ever is comfortable for them.

■ Looking after yourself

Present the idea

Practical action: ask them to think about something they could do for themselves.

Session 2: Beginnings

Facilitator notes

Setting the scene

- Make sure you've typed out ground rules to give out this week.
- **Handout 3** The maze

  Handout 4 Social Model of disability
- Remember that at the end of this session you need to allow time to ask the group what they would like their presentation on next week.
- Chocolate for prizes (the maze exercise)
- Flipchart and pens

Key points for facilitators

Material

The diagnosis process

Even after a number of years, telling the story of diagnosis can still be traumatic, it therefore has some potential to introduce some powerful emotions into the groups fairly early on.

The maze

This is designed to make the point about having to tell your story over and over again to many professionals, but also to establish laughter and enjoying yourself as something that happens in this group/course.

Social and Medical Model of disability

Presented well this can be a powerful first step to parents moving on. A key issue with this as far as parenting is concerned is the one where you 'Go in with a child and come out with a label', getting rid of the idea that professionals know more than parents do about their own children.

Group dynamics

A really important part of what a facilitator must do early on is to ensure that the group feel safe enough for members to take personal risks. One of the essential ways of doing this is to make sure the structures in the group stay in place. If group members don't like the structure in place or the course content there can be flexibility for that to change but there must be some sort of structure in place. A facilitator must monitor how the group are coping with the planned structure. If the group members don't own it and use it to take personal risks then it isn't really working. I know that when I talk too much there are too many silences and one-word answers. At this point, it's time to review and change things.

Running order

- **Off-load time**
- **Storytelling and listening**

  Experiences of the diagnosis process

- **Something funny**

  The maze exercise

This is a whole-group exercise and is designed to be as light hearted and funny as possible. Flipchart the maze and follow it through with each parent. For every professional that they have visited they receive a token, the parent who has seen the most receives a prize, and the parent who knows what they all do receives one too. Chocolate makes good prizes! Give out copies of **Handout 3** The maze.

- **Something to learn**

  Medical Model of disability

Use material from Chapter 1 'Beginnings' to do a short presentation on the history of the Medical Model.
  Mention:

- Where it comes from – a bit about history
- How it can affects parents – at diagnosis parenting becomes public, you often don't get any help, and you go in with a child and come out with a label.
- **Feelings check**

  In small groups discuss:

How do I feel about my child having a disability?

■ Something to learn

Social Model of disability

Again use material from Chapter 1 'Beginnings' for a short presentation on the history and implications for parents of the Social Model of disability. Give out copies of **Handout 4** Social Model of disability.

■ Feelings check

How do I feel about my child?

■ Practical action

What do I need to do about

finding my way around the maze?

getting a diagnosis?

Split into small groups and brainstorm the question most appropriate to them and then feedback to the rest of the group.

■ Looking after yourself

Exercise in pairs: plan an activity for yourself to be done by next week between 10–30 minutes in length.

■ Looking forward

Thoughts on next week – Choose your information subject

Choose between 'A whistle-stop tour of the education system for children with special needs' and 'A whistle-stop tour of the financial help for parents with a child with special needs'.

Session 3: Building up support

Facilitator notes

Setting the scene

- Preparations – Of all the sessions this one requires the most organisation in advance. Don't worry if you can't do all of this for week 3. You could have resources and information available each week for parents to look at. You need to gather the following information:

  - *Financial support* – If possible before this session contact your local carers association or see the Resource directory (for national phone numbers) for sample copies of: Disability Living Allowance, Invalid Carers Allowance and Family Fund. Contact your local health visitor for details about how to apply for free nappies in your area.

  - *Support groups* – Before the session, check through group member enrolment forms to make sure you have the details of their children's special needs. Then using the Resource directory make a list of relevant national and, if possible, local support groups, including websites. (The local support groups may take a little more investigation; checking in the local press or local council may help, Contact a Family may help too.) There are also generic national groups such as Mencap, Afasic and again Contact a Family, which are very useful if the child has been given a general diagnosis such as 'Moderate Learning Difficulties' or 'Global Speech and Language Disorder' or no diagnosis at all.

  - *Leisure opportunities* – Check with the Disabled Children's Team of your local social services to see how after-school provision for children with special needs is organised in your area and find out the criteria and procedure for obtaining respite care. Also check in the local press and with local voluntary agencies, such as Barnardos and Mencap, to see what their provision is. There are often leisure opportunities such as swimming clubs for children with special needs which are useful to know about. National organisations such as the National Autistic Society provide schemes such as 'Parent to Parent' and Befriending, which provide active support (see Resource directory for contact details).

    – *Education advice* – Get in touch with your local Parent Partnership organisation or any other local education advisory service and see if they can provide you with leaflets and information about what they are able to offer.

- **Handout 5** The education process

    Handout 6 Education terms

    Handout 7 Benefits

    Handout 8 Signposts

- Chocolate for Signposts game!

Key points for facilitators

Material

Presenting information

Balance is key in this session. This is an information-led session but as a facilitator you need to remember that this is not a presentation but a group. Let the parents determine how much information they receive this week. It may well be overwhelming for parents to receive this all at once anyway. Use your judgement; it may be possible to give information gradually over the weeks as you accumulate it.

How parents feel about receiving support

It's a huge shift in your view of yourself as a parent to move towards interdependence and ask for help. Mentioning it for the first time is likely to produce a whole range of difficult emotions: anger, a sense of failure, guilt and shame.

Building up support

This is designed to be an overview, to get parents to think, possibly for the first time, about support for themselves and their families.

    A key aspect of this is the relationship with professionals. Introduce the idea during the discussion that it is possible to work towards an effective partnership with professionals as part of receiving support. This needs to be gently introduced and returned to at a later point.

Group dynamics

When something happens to an individual group member, or she or he makes a revealing comment, it can be a real opportunity for the group to move on and become more cohesive. For example, someone may cry and then tell a really distressing story. There are many benefits to this if this is handled well and sensitively facilitated. The group member will feel better for crying, others will have the opportunity to connect and share their stories and everyone will have learned that in this group tears are accepted.

Follow up

There may be a number of referrals here so at least have a list to give out to parents of organisations and phone numbers who can help. There will either be specific needs like benefit advice or educational advice, or it will be apparent that a more general overview for family support is needed. In which case help the parent apply to social services for a carer's assessment. If you are not able to do this, refer the parent to a voluntary or government funded agency who can help the family through this process, for example Sure Start, Mencap Family Advisor service or the local Carers Association.

Running order

- **Off-load time**
- **Storytelling and listening**

  Parents tell their stories about the support they receive.

- **Something funny**

  Signposts game. Where do I go to get . . .?

Small group exercise: in small groups, using **Handout 8** Signposts ask questions like, 'Who do I go to get free nappies?'. Use chocolate as prizes.

- **Something to learn**

  Choice of information subject: education or financial help?

Give out copies of relevant handouts, for education use **Handout 5** The education process and **Handout 6** Education terms and for financial help use **Handout 7** Benefits.

- **Feelings check**

  How do I feel about getting support?

This is a whole-group discussion that needs to be handled sensitively. Most parents are surviving difficult situations and you do not want to undermine how well they are managing. The concept of having practical and financial help may be something that they have just not thought about before. Also this is a very early stage in the group and they may not want to disclose how difficult life is at times. Finally, there will be a strong underlying feeling of guilt that somehow they should cope and by asking for support they are admitting failure.

- **Something to learn**

  Concept of interdependence

Do a short presentation using material from Chapter 2 'Building up support' on why it's logical and reasonable not to do everything for yourself.

■ **Practical action**

Building up my support

In pairs consider the gaps in your support network; encourage parents to look at relationships.

Feedback to the whole group.

Whole-group question: How would positive relationships with professionals help? How might that happen?

■ **Looking after yourself**

Review whether anyone did do a 'looking after yourself' activity last week. Then in small groups ask them what they liked doing before they had children. Ask them each to come up with an achievable, realistic 'looking after themselves' activity and do it by next week.

■ **Looking forward**

What sort of communication difficulties do your children have?

Session 4: Communication and relationship building

Facilitator notes

Setting the scene

■ Preparations – Develop a relationship with the local speech and language service. Often, they run workshops or short courses in partnership with others on various communication techniques, so finding out when they are in advance would be a good idea.

■ **Handout 9** The communication process

  Handout 10 Ways of helping with communication

  Handout 11 Communication alternatives

There may be comments and feedback that parents have given, and which have been put on the flipchart; these can usefully be made into handouts.

  Not all these handouts need to be given out, it depends on the audience. You may want some available for parents to look at on a resource table.

Key points for facilitators

Material

Communication is complex for anyone to understand. This session will only be a beginning to that, but the aim is to meet parents where they are. Not being able to communicate with your child for whatever reason causes lots of feelings of guilt and powerlessness, those feelings need to be acknowledged.
Key issues:

Communication is more than words

If you really can't bear to do role-play don't but it's fun to try! The object of the exercise is to rethink what parents mean by communication, to see it in as wide a context as possible.

The communication process

Don't worry when you do the presentation about getting every detail precise; this is not a lecture, it is an overview, an introduction. If parents want to learn more about it they can go on courses about communication. The practical action section here has to be well facilitated, as this could be a really depressing process where parents simply identify what their child is not doing. Make the point that if your child is not speaking, she is simply communicating at an early stage of development, she is not doing anything wrong.

Feelings

As you can see from my account in the book (Chapter 3 'Communication and relationship building') communication difficulties can cause parents a lot of anguish and distress. This may be the first time they've realised how they feel about it. So this has to be handled very sensitively. If you are getting a lot of guilt expressed remind them that whatever stage the child is at in communication terms, he is not doing anything wrong; it's not the child's fault nor is it the parents' fault.

Parents' style of communication

This section is more critical than the practical action section that looks at communication strategies because this focuses on what is going on for parents internally.

This has to be done in an atmosphere of complete acceptance. It's also really important to take this at parents' own pace.

Communication strategies

The important issue regarding this section is that it meets parents' needs practically. It should be an opportunity to brainstorm so that parents go away with some practical strategies that will work for them at home. This is likely to be done in small groups and means that both facilitators give each group member equal time and no one person should monopolise the space.

Group dynamics

A danger is when a group is exposed to terrible pain, anxiety or anger from another group member too early on – 'too much too soon'. That's why having a debriefing session and having a co-facilitator to talk to are both so important; work out who your vulnerable group members are and how you are going to mange their internal distress before it erupts.

However, if it does happen, and sometimes it's not possible to prevent it, bear in mind the key principle of facilitation: to avoid doing harm. So go for low-level intervention rather than high-risk challenging or attacking comments. It is better to talk about underlying fears in an indirect comment such as, 'It's really difficult to cope when your kids get in trouble at school,' than say something like, 'Everyone is really quiet today,' in a direct attacking way. With the person who is overexposed it is always better to make gentle challenges and boundary setting rather than aggressive controlling comments. Therefore it is much better to listen respectfully and then say 'Joe that experience sounds awful, we really appreciate you telling us and off-load time is coming to an end now, are you OK for us to move on?'

Running order

- **Off-load time**

- **Storytelling and listening**

  Experiences of communicating with your child

This is designed to focus on how parents feel about communicating with their child.

- **Something funny**

  How we communicate–Communication scenarios that show what goes on without words

Role-play with your co-facilitators some simple scenarios to the rest of the group (the more humorous and exaggerated the better). Here are two examples but feel free to think your own up!

Scenario 1: Parent and child

Parent: What have you been up to?
Child goes to answer. Parent doesn't give her time.
Parent: You don't have to tell me, I can see you've been up to no good. Well you can wipe that smile off your face for a start.
Child looks puzzled and tries to wipe smile off her face with a cloth.
Parent: What are you doing? Honestly and for goodness sake, make sure you wipe you feet on that mat.
Child really puzzled now, but scratching her head takes her shoes and socks off and wipes her feet.

Scenario 2: Two friends speaking

Sarah: So how you?
Katie: I'm fine.
Katie looks far from fine, her arms are folded really stiffly, she looks really upset and every so often she's dabbing her eyes with a hanky.
Sarah: Oh that's OK then, so can you pick Susie up for me? Here's her bag and lunch money and she needs to give this letter to her teacher.
Sarah hands all these things to Katie who looks on in disbelief.
Sarah goes.
Katie picks up the phone: I am never going to help that Sarah ever again. She is so selfish; you'll never guess what happened when she came round . . .

When both scenarios are completed ask the group what they think the communication problems were. Make the point that children's speech and language difficulties are not just restricted to not speaking but they are many and varied.

■ Something To learn

A whistle-stop tour of communication

A brief presentation on communication development from the earliest stages. At each stage note what should happen and the problems that can occur. Think about your audience when you're planning the presentation. Give out copies of **Handout 9** The communication process.

■ Practical action

Being a detective

In small groups and using **Handout 9** provided, parents can identify where their child is developmentally when it comes to communication.

■ Feelings check

In pairs

What happens to my relationship with my child because of the communication difficulties? How do I feel about it?

■ Something to learn

Communication styles

Split into two groups, one group makes a list of positive ways of communicating with children and the other negative ways. Feedback to the whole group (see Chapter 3 'Communication and relationship building' the styles of communication section). Then ask the group what might happen to children when they're spoken to negatively or positively.

■ Feelings check

In pairs, discuss what we are feeling when we communicate negatively and positively with our children.

■ Practical action: sharing ideas

Developing ideas for building up my relationship with my child

Communication ideas – In small groups ask parents what ideas and strategies they have that help their relationship with their child and increase communication. Feedback to the whole group and use the ideas to develop a practical list of ideas to try at home, incorporating other ideas from **Handout 10** Ways of helping with communication.

■ Looking after yourself

Review 'looking after yourselves' activities that parents managed last week. This week each group member should continue the 10–30 minutes doing something for themselves and also think of two positive qualities they have as a parent.

Session 5: Behaviour

Facilitator notes

Setting the scene

- **Handout 12** Iceberg model

  Handout 13 Stimuli/belief/response

  Handout 14 Belief systems

  Handout 15 Behaviour toolkit

  Handout 16 Behaviour stressbusting

- Practical points – Finish on time. Experience as a facilitator tells me that this is a really hard session to finish because often people want to go on discussing things. Apart from key practical considerations finishing on time makes people feel safe.

Key points for facilitators

Material

Sensitivity

This is the key word for this session. Parents who have children with special needs feel guilty enough already. It is very important in this session to use careful self-disclosure; talk about your own experience as a parent or a professional working with children.

'They all do it'

The key message behind storytelling and something funny is most children with special needs at one time or another get into behaviour that is either mystifying, frustrating or even frightening. It's to disconnect parents from the idea that they are doing something wrong and are therefore bad parents. Once you've done that you can move on to what really causes difficult behaviour.

Being a detective

Using the iceberg model, make this as interactive as possible. The more parents' real life examples you use the better. Also use the checklist of things that might affect behaviour (see Trigger Points on p. 73). This is about discovery, finding out what messages children are giving us through their behaviour.

Belief systems

This is one of the most challenging sections in this course; it will be demanding for parents to take part and some may choose not to, while others may feel afterwards that they've said too much and therefore feel vulnerable. So again, careful facilitation and good use of self-disclosure here helps to show how your responses have been affected by your beliefs. The section will often bring a discussion about culture, especially those cultures that believe that punishment is the answer. Allow discussion to go that way and use the book to help you. However, be careful that any discussion, however interesting, does not sidetrack you from the issues you need to cover.

Behaviour strategies

The key item in the Finding the truth exercise (Practical action 1) is considering ways of changing peoples' beliefs about themselves. This is actually more important than any of the strategies that follow; parents have to believe they can change things for things to change. This needs time.

Behaviour toolbox: Although this practical action exercise is done as a presentation, it needs to be as interactive as possible. It is good to start with a quick pair exercise where parents name their most effective way of dealing with difficult behaviour. The way you present the toolkit depends on the nature of the children's disabilities represented; use general ideas and then those that are most appropriate.

Group dynamics

This session is asking more of parents in terms of disclosure and reflection. This is often the time when more group resistance can occur. Group resistance or defence mechanisms are ways people find of feeling safe within groups. Some examples of defence mechanisms are:

Intellectualising – talking about something factually without any real emotion attached. This is an early defence.

All comments are directed at the facilitator – another early defence where group members are too scared to talk to each other.

Over-exposure of one person – so everyone else feels safe and then tries to 'fix' that person's problems.

Challenge the value of the group and the ability of the facilitator

Side talking – talk to your neighbour but not to the rest of the group.

Talk about someone else's problems who isn't there.

Deny you have any problems of your own.

The way to deal with these issues is if defence mechanisms occur in the early stages allow them unless they are very dangerous, for example likely to harm someone or cause the structure of the group to break down. To stay, people need to feel safe and you want people to stay. However, if defence mechanisms have become a way of life to the group and that's all they do, you need to intervene to get things back on track. Another good reason for intervening is if you can see that some people feel safe enough to want to work and move on and don't need the defence mechanism any more.

Follow up

Local health authorities, social services and education authorities often have professionals who can help with behavioural issues (check Resource directory for details).

Running order

- **Off-load time**
- **Storytelling and listening**

    My stories about behaviour

Parents' experiences – an opportunity for parents to share their experiences of their child's behaviour.

- **Something funny**

    Vote on your funniest story

This is exactly what it says. Our children do the most unexpected and frankly hysterical things so encourage the group to vote for the funniest story.

- **Something to learn**

    Working out what's going on – the iceberg model

The iceberg model – The idea behind this concept is becoming a detective; what is the child's behaviour telling you? Part of this detective process is each parent under-standing something about their child's condition and how a affects their behaviour. This model needs to be introduced on the flipchart then looked at in small groups. Like any good detective each parent will be given tools: a handout about the children's different conditions, the checklist about factors that might affect behaviour and

Handout 12 Iceberg model. Ask parents to chose a particular behaviour that's annoying them about their child at the moment and in pairs, using their tools, work out what's going on.

■ Feelings check

Why is my child's behaviour so difficult to deal with?

How does my child's behaviour make me feel?

How does my child's behaviour make me feel about being a parent?

■ Something to learn

Introduce the concept of stimuli/belief/response (give out copies of **Handout 13** Stimuli/belief/response).

Stimuli are the child's behaviour – what's going on 'out there'.
Belief is what you feel and believe about that behaviour. Examples are:

'I'm a useless parent and there is nothing I can do that will change anything.'

'I daren't change anything at home, if I do all hell will break loose.'

'The problem is this child's behaviour, I'm going to punish him so badly, and he won't know what's hit him.'

'This child is deliberately trying to hurt me.'

Response is how your beliefs cause you to respond to the behaviour.

Small group exercise: In two groups, using **Handout 14** Belief systems, ask parents what sort of responses are likely when you believe such things about yourself and your child. It is useful to give parents some scenarios to work from.

■ Practical action (1)

Finding the truth

In pairs get parents to come up with some beliefs about themselves and their children, such as '*I am the expert here.*'

■ Practical action (2)

Making a behaviour toolkit

This is whole-group exercise using the ideas from the book to create a behaviour toolkit. The toolkit is a collection of ideas of things that might help. It is not designed as the complete solution to dealing with difficult behaviour, but as a beginning to help parents develop their own ideas for what would work in their own family settings.

A good way to start this is encouraging parents to ask themselves 'What works for me already?' Give out copies of **Handout 15** Behaviour toolkit.

■ Looking after yourself

Review what 'looking after yourselves' activities people have managed to do this last week.

Ask parents to use the two positive parenting qualities they thought of last week to create some new belief systems about themselves. Continue with a 'looking after yourself' activity of 10–30 minutes. Finally, if they have any time at all, ask them to try out the suggestions on **Handout 16** Behaviour stressbusting. This looks at children's behaviour from the perspective of how much stress it is causing you.

Session 6: Stress

Facilitator notes

Setting the scene

- **Handouts 17** Stress
  Handout 18 Post-traumatic stress disorder
  Handout 19 'Perfect' parent and child
  Handout 20 Stressbusting kit
- Flipchart

Key points for facilitators

Material

Picture of stress

The key issue in this session is helping parents to get a true picture or perspective on how much stress they're under. There is a sense in which because you're just surviving day to day as a parent of a child with a disability you have no time to stop and reflect on what is going on. Therefore it is very likely to be a shock to people. The other part to this as a parent is that you don't really want to know how difficult things really are because your fear is that you just won't be able to cope. So there'll be resistance to looking at this. So how do you handle this as a facilitator? Don't patronise. Treat their amazing ability to manage with dignity and respect. This is a case of saying, yes you are incredible and let's start to look at ways to make your life more than survival. You deserve to live a good life.

Something to learn (1) and (2)

Choose which is more appropriate to your group: if you have a group of parents who you would describe as in the main being in a state of chronic stress, then I would do (1); if the group of parents are experiencing milder stress I would do (2). The reason behind (2) is the amount of stress tied up in expectations is substantial; letting go of at least some of them could have a dramatic effect on someone's life.

Group dynamics

By this time the group may well have reached a stage in a group's life sometimes called the '**norming**' group.

At this stage there is more energy to do some work and members feel less anxious and more secure. People will not have stayed unless they are getting a personal payoff and to get that they will have had to have taken a risk and exposed themselves to danger. Defence mechanisms are beginning to decrease. The group has found ways of feeling safe without having to resort to them on quite so many occasions. However, there can be events which are just too big for the group to manage and then the facilitator needs to intervene. This is the stage where group members begin to enjoy **group cohesiveness** – a sense of belonging to the group and the feeling that the group is a good place to be.

Running order

- **Off-load time**
- **Storytelling and listening**

    Stories about my life, 'If they knew the half of it . . .'

Very often people make comments to parents that show that they have no idea what life is like for a parent of a child with special needs. This is an opportunity to tell their stories of the sort of stress they go through.

- **Something funny**

    Things that could only happen to me

This is a time to discuss the bizarre situations we find ourselves in, stressful at the time, funny afterwards.

- **Something to learn**

    Start with a whole group exercise about the sort of stress this group of parents is under (see Chapter 5 'Stress' for ideas). Brainstorm ideas on the flipchart.

- **Feelings check**

    Get each parent to create their own picture of how it is for them. Fill out **Handout 17** Stress and ask them to be as honest as possible.

- **Something to learn (1)**

    Taking a look at post-traumatic stress disorder

Do a mini presentation on this disorder using the same categories: feelings, physical reactions, actions. Give out copies of **Handout 18** Post-traumatic stress disorder. Compare this with what parents wrote on their handout (**Handout 17**).

■ Something to learn (2)

Looking at expectations

Expectations cause stress – Where do they come from?

This exercise can be done on the flipchart; a drawing of a parent and child is useful. What does society expect a perfect parent and child to be like? A good way into this exercise is by asking the parents to think of someone they think of as nearly perfect as a parent. What are they like and what's their child like? Give out copies of **Handout 19** 'Perfect' parent and child.

Now, in pairs discuss the idea of being good enough rather than perfect.

Follow this by thinking about expectations about being the perfect family. What was expected of us when we were children? How does that affect us as adults? Feedback using the flipchart to the whole group.

The final expectation to consider is my future. As parents, having a child with a disability, may have completely changed what I feel I can do with my own life. Use the feelings check to explore this.

■ Feelings check

How does it feel living my life?

Do this as a pairs exercise.

■ Practical action

Developing a stressbusting kit

Start off by getting some ideas from the group. Then use the ideas from Chapter 5 'Stress' in the book. Particularly emphasise looking after yourself as a 'state of mind' and asking for help. Give out copies of **Handout 20** Stressbusting kit.

■ Looking after yourself

Review last week's activities and see if anyone used **Handout 16** Behaviour stressbusting. Encourage parents to use it as a way of dealing with stress. This week parents should continue to think about extending their 'looking after themselves' activity to one hour (even if they have to do two 30 minutes slots). Also think about the idea of looking after yourself as a 'state of mind'. How can they make that happen for themselves?

Session 7: Facing the feelings

Facilitator notes

Setting the scene

- **Handout 21** Cycle of emotions
  Handout 22 Feelings list
- You may need tissues for this session.

Key points for facilitators

Material

The key to this session is allowing people to talk and identify how they feel. Not everybody will want or be ready to do this and you need to be sensitive to that in your planning and facilitation. The important issue is to have enough structure and boundaries to make people feel safe, but not so much that parent's ability to work things through is drowned out.

Cycle of emotions

It is called a cycle because it does not have a beginning, middle or end; it is possible to re-visit emotions again and again. It is in fact a lifelong adjustment process.

Shame and guilt

It is important not to force disclosure but at the same time to be aware of what is going on below the surface and if appropriate, generally comment. These feelings can range from feeling guilty that the child wasn't diagnosed sooner to feeling shame that a parent wished the child in question was dead.

The difference between sadness and depression

Sadness is a series of emotions, thoughts and behaviours connected to loss. Depression is an illness or mood disorder, which can be connected to actual events or for which the cause is not known. Another key difference is that deep sadness often leads someone on to greater quest for meaning, in this search hope and acceptance are often found. This is not usually the case with someone suffering from depression.

Group dynamics

Self-awareness as a facilitator

Your feelings are very important. They are a way in to understanding other people's feelings and understanding what's going on in the whole group. They should never be ignored. If they are, they can cause problems in the group.

What are you likely to feel? Before the group begins, you'll have certain hopes and fears about how the group will work out. Once the group starts, certain events will stir up feelings from your past and if you are a parent with a child with special needs this will be particularly true. You need to be careful that your own feelings don't get in the way of what is going on in the group, so you can continue to be useful. Powerful feelings are bound to be stirred up and that makes de-brief and supervision essential.

Name the unnameable

Say what is on everyone else's mind but feel they can't say. It is particularly useful in a group with parents of children with disabilities to name the emotions that are there in the room but people can't talk about, such as anger and shame. However, this sort of intervention can only happen in the norming or performing stage in the group. This is one of the points where it's really useful that one of your facilitators has children with special needs and can therefore speak from experience.

Follow up

This is obviously a session that will raise feelings for many parents. Some parents will simply need time to process, but if a parent is particularly distressed a referral to an agency such as Sure Start or voluntary agencies such as Homestart or Family Welfare Association may be appropriate to give the parent extra support.

Running order

- **Off-load time**
- **Storytelling and listening**

  Why is it so hard to talk about how I feel?

Ask parents to talk about why they think it's much easier to talk about what we do rather than how we feel about it.

- **Something to learn**

  The cycle of feelings we face

This is a presentation using **Handout 21** Cycle of emotions demonstrating the kind of feelings faced.

■ **Feelings check**

There are two ways of doing this exercise. One is by using a list of words provided (**Handout 22** Feelings list) and asking parents to work out which feelings apply to them. The other would be to give the parents main headings such as anger, guilt, denial, etc. and in small groups ask them to come up with a word that best describes how they feel. For example, for anger they might say frustrated, for shame, ashamed.

■ **Storytelling and listening**

Naming our feelings

Ask the parents to take the feelings they've described, and talk about times when they have felt these different feelings with or about their child.

■ **Something to learn**

In the whole group, brainstorm why it's really important to express feelings. Follow the usual process of letting ideas come from parents first, then using material from the book (Chapter 6 'The emotional journey: facing the feelings') and your own life experience broaden the discussion.

■ **Practical action**

Always when feelings are expressed the fear is how am I going to manage? So in small groups that are carefully facilitated, talk about ways of dealing with hard times when you feel terrible. If the groups have time, develop the discussion to include 'things to do when I'm feeling angry/sad/guilty . . .'.

■ **Something funny**

Why am I laughing now?

If you can, let there be a time here when parents talk about how they found themselves laughing even in the most difficult situations.

■ **Looking after yourself**

Review last week's activities and what they thought about 'looking after themselves' as a state of mind. This week is called 'looking after yourself as a way of life'; the idea is to plan preferably a day, or half a day, of something for them. In pairs encourage them to dream, what would they do with that day? Also remind them to continue with the weekly time for themselves, hopefully between 30 minutes to an hour.

Session 8: Families

Facilitator notes

Setting the scene

- **Handout 23** Cycle of behaviour

  Handout 24 Problem solving

  Handout 25 Family moving-on kit

- Preparations – Check up on family support in the area before this session. Useful information would be details of local counselling services for individuals, couples and families, sibling support groups (for siblings of children with special needs) and local agencies and charities that work with the whole family.

- Extra pens and paper
- Flipchart

Key points for facilitators

Material

Looking at the whole family

It may be the first time these parents have ever realised the whole picture. The key issue in this session is to get the focus off the child with a disability and on to the whole family. The basic premise is that if the family thrives, the child will too.

Family's needs

I think this 'something to learn' exercise, if well facilitated, can produce some really illuminating results. Again, expect resistance as you are asking parents to reflect on an issue that they rarely if ever consider. There could be a lot of guilt again here too.

Cycle of behaviour/problem solving

This is to get away from either a blame culture ('It's all this persons' fault,') or a victim fatalistic culture ('There's nothing we can do to change anything,') and move to a realistic pragmatic place that says, 'We all contribute to what goes on in our family and if we stand back we'll be able to see what is going on and then we will be able to find some solutions.'

Family moving-on kit

This is about careful facilitation to produce brainstorming that results in practical and realistic ways to move on.

Group dynamics

It is likely that by this session the group reaches a stage where members are feeling angry and trying to manage that anger. It has become a '**storming**' group. There is much to be angry about in the issues being discussed, but also there will be some group concerns. They are likely to be concerned about how much power they have in the group and whether they or the facilitator have the control. This period of anger is often productive; out of it often comes the period when the group does the most work, the '**performing**' group.

   In the light of this, it's useful to consider the sort of dangers that facilitators should avoid:

- talking too much;

- talking to one person for too long so it becomes a conversation rather than a group discussion;

- agreeing to change something without thinking and not giving the original material and structure enough time; alternatively

- holding on to your planned structure and group content when it becomes obvious no one is joining in;

- having a style of facilitation that is aggressive, controlling and over managing;

- colluding – going along with a defence mechanism and getting caught up in it;

- favouritism – finding one person more interesting than the others. This can have terrible consequences and may cause the group to scapegoat the favourite. Because being in a group is very like a family, favouritism causes group members to feel abandoned and unsupported. It's really important that everyone gets enough attention and are never ignored.

How do you deal with mistakes? Some mistakes can just be acknowledged: 'I've been talking too much, I'm going to stop now.' This shows that everyone can make mistakes but that the facilitator still accepts him or herself. In the case of collusion, just stop colluding. In the case of favouritism it is more tricky. Try to give attention to all the other members in the group and then later on in de-brief work out why it happened.

Running order

■ **Off-load time**

■ **Exercise**

Who makes up your family?

All families are very different. Ask parents when they think of the word 'family' who do they think of?

■ **Storytelling and listening**

Family stories

Encourage group members to talk about the relationships that are important in their life. Then talk about the effect that their child with special needs has on these relationships.

■ **Something funny**

When do you and your family really laugh? When do you have fun?

■ **Something to learn**

Mums, dads, brothers, sisters and grandparents – What's going on for them? What do they all need?

This is a small group exercise. Give one group 'Dads and Partner relationship' and one group, 'Other children and mums'. Give them large sheets of paper divided down the middle, and on one side put 'Positive' and on the other side put 'Negative'. Then ask them to fill in what was positive and negative for these different groups about being in a family with a child with a disability.

Feedback on the flipchart and add relevant points from the book (Chapter 7 'Families') and your own experience.

■ **Feelings check**

Working in pairs consider: How do you feel about the other relationships in your life?

■ **Something to learn**

Cycle of behaviour

The idea behind this concept of the cycle of behaviour is to help parents look at how they and their family respond to their child with special needs' behaviour and how this becomes a cycle of behaviour within the family with its own momentum.

Do a small group exercise using the cycle of behaviour (**Handout 23**) and also introduce the idea of problem solving – standing back and observing (**Handout 24**). Use a scenario that demonstrates the cycle of behaviour and consider:

What needs are being expressed here?

Whose needs need meeting/addressing first?

What is going to help this family?

The best scenarios to use are the ones parents bring themselves. However if none is forthcoming use the following scenario.

Waqis is an eight-year-old boy with Asperger's syndrome and ADHD. His little brother Abdul who is five wants to play, so he won't leave him alone. Abdul is teasing him and keeps taking his cars away from him. Abdul is making a lot of noise. Waqis gets really frustrated and bites Abdul who immediately starts screaming. His mother Nazneen runs in from the kitchen to see what's going on. Abdul is carrying on screaming but shows her bite marks. Nazneen shouts at Waqis who starts crying, at which point his father, Omar, walks in and hearing Nazneen shout at Waqis tells her off. Nazneen is really angry with Omar so shouts back at him.

■ Practical action

In the same small groups using their problem-solving skills and **Handout 25** Family moving-on kit, go back to the flipchart and see if they can come up with some solutions to the negative issues that mums, dads, other children and partners' relationships face. These solutions should be as practical as possible.

■ Looking after yourself

Review last week's activities and then continue 'looking after yourself as a way of life' by getting back into the pairs they had last week. Review their dreams for a day or half a day, 'looking after themselves' time. Then, on a sheet of paper write down the barriers to this happening. Collect up the papers at the end for use in Session 9. Remind parents to continue their normal 'looking after themselves' activities.

Session 9: Hope

Facilitator notes

Setting the scene

- **Handout 26** Barriers to hope

  Handout 27 Relationship web
- Extra pens and paper
- Flipchart

Key points for facilitators

Material

Barriers to hope

This exercise involves filling in a picture of a brick wall. The key issue behind this session, and one that it is worth emphasising, is how do we break down the brick walls in our lives? Having completed this exercise it may be worth doing a flipchart presentation about the barriers. They fall into the following categories:

- Internal – Our belief systems, culture, fears and anxieties, styles of communication. Some of the ways of breaking down this barrier is challenging what we have always believed and changing our style of communication (hence the need for assertiveness).
- External – Lack of knowledge (hence needing to know the system) and hard work (need the support of others, hence circle of support or support groups).

Therefore this exercise is not meant to lead to feeling hopeless but the beginning of change. It may be really important to do the presentation just to restore hope.

Relationship web

The same can be said for this exercise, which is not designed to cause parents to feel terrible but to help them see the importance of building up support and reducing isolation. You cannot prevent parents feeling hopeless or bleak, but you can impress on them that it is well within their power to gain support and move on.

Group dynamics

As groups progress, a number of difficult issues can occur. These include:

- Scapegoating – One person is being verbally attacked, criticised or blamed by most of the others. It is a defence mechanism; everyone is protected except the one who is attacked. The facilitator must always intervene because this could be very destructive. The best intervention from the facilitator is to use general comments thereby taking the heat away from the person being scapegoated. Name unnameable feelings and fears that are causing this attack. Very often, scapegoating happens because the group is angry with the facilitator and actually needs the opportunity to express that anger directly.

- Anxious questioning – When parents ask a lot of anxious questions, answer them factually and neutrally; this gets fears out in the open and deals with them.

- Absences – These need checking out to find out whether the parent is all right and particularly whether this person feels personally damaged by something you may not have picked up.

Running order

- **Off-load time**
- **Storytelling and listening**

    What I do to get me through

    Parents' stories of how things they do or think help them get through and move on.

- **Something funny**

    Things that make me laugh and get me through

- **Something to learn**

    Barriers to hope – What are my barriers to hope?

    To move on, things need to change.

    In small groups discuss what stops people moving on; their children and themselves. Using **Handout 26** Barriers to hope find out what are their barriers to things changing.

- **Feelings check**

    How do I feel about being hopeful?

    Hope is a dangerous emotion. How do parents feel about it?

■ Something to learn

Ways through (1)

Knowing the system

Give a brief presentation about getting around the system, followed by a longer role-play. This time it would be really good if you could get two parents involved.

The situation

School: Teacher has asked parent in because child Rosie, aged seven, is getting into trouble. Teacher thinks she's just naughty, yet Rosie already has a speech and language disorder and dyspraxia. Parent needs to help the teacher understand that Rosie's behaviour is to do with her difficulties.

You can either get a brave parent to play both parts or preferably two parents. The rest of the group should be observers; one of the facilitators could be the teacher.

Scenario 1: Rosie's mum, Carol, is passive

Teacher: 'Well I'm really concerned about Rosie's behaviour.'
Carol: very respectful, speaks with no confidence, wants to agree with the teacher to keep the peace, is very nice.
What does Carol do?

When the role-play is over ask the parent who is playing Carol how she might have been feeling inside and how she was left feeling. Ask the parent or facilitator who played the teacher how the teacher felt and then open it out to the group – what do they think Carol felt at the time and afterwards?

Scenario 2: Rosie's mum, Carol, is aggressive

Teacher: asks the same question
Carol: not respectful, interrupts, hostile, sits with arms folded and glares at the teacher.
What does Carol do?

When the role-play is over, ask the same questions as the previous time.

Scenario 3: Rosie's mum, Carol, is assertive

Teacher: asks the same question
Carol: respectful, calm, confident, looks the teacher straight in the eye. She is expecting to have a conversation not a confrontation.
What does Carol do?

Again, ask the same questions and then draw the discussion together with some general points about the differences between passivity, aggression and assertiveness.

■ Practical action

This is a small group exercise. Ask two questions:

What is stopping me getting into the system and getting things done for my family and me?

What is stopping me being assertive?

■ Something learn

Relationship web exercise

Use **Handout 27** Relationship web and explain:

Inner circle: our most intimate relationships

Second circle: friends

Third circle: acquaintances

Outer circle: People who I pay/who are paid for being in my life

After a short presentation, get each parent to fill in their handout individually.

■ Practical action

How can I make more support happen?

■ Looking after yourself

Review last week's activities. Then take the written sheets from last week, 'Barriers to looking after yourself' and in small groups ask parents to share ideas as to how those barriers can be broken.

Session 10: Facing the future

Setting the scene

- **Handout 28** A different view of myself

  Handout 29 A different view of my child

- Preparations – This is the last week of the course and needs to be a celebration. Parents may already be bringing food but you may want to supplement that. Some acknowledgement is also a good idea, for example certificates give people a rightful sense of achievement.

- Feedback – It's useful to think in advance what you've valued about the group as a whole and each individual member so you can give them that verbal feedback. This can mean a great deal to parents and is well worth the time and effort.

Key points for facilitators

Material

Dreaming

Part of the MAPs process (see Chapter 8 'Hope' of the book for details) from the Inclusion movement is encouraging people to dream. Dreaming is where our hopes for the future are located. It's a dangerous but ultimately life-giving process. This needs sensitive facilitation and note that this could be a beginning of something very different and that it's good to dream with others in circles of support so change can occur.

A different view of myself

Encourage parents to be as specific as possible here.

A different view of my child

This exercise can be absolutely wonderful. If parents have attended the whole course they will be ready to write to their child. The letter can be about their hopes and dreams for this child's future as well as what they think of him or her in the present.

Evaluation

It is important to leave time for this, because you as a facilitator will find this incredibly helpful.

Summarise

Pull all the threads together and reflect on the journey people have made and their hopes for the future. It is useful to make some comments about endings and how people may be feeling about the last session.

Group dynamics

This is the stage, often referred to as the '**performing**' group, when members have the most trust for each other and are working the hardest. It is likely to be the time when they may want to start to explore what they want out of life and what they are most scared of – their hopes and fears. However it is also the time members are preoccupied with the end of the group; feelings of loss are emerging. Endings are difficult, especially if group members have had past experiences of loss and abandonment and separation.

Follow up

It may be possible, in partnership with others, to offer parents an ongoing support group with a facilitator; that is the ideal to follow a course like this and will enable parents to revisit many of the themes already touched on the course. However, if that is not possible, here are some ideas of future follow ups:

1 At the very least encourage parents to set up a network of support between them, swapping addresses and phone numbers.

2 Consider the possibility of helping them find a venue so that they can meet together on their own.

3 Organise regular follow-up meetings with you or a colleague, perhaps once or twice a term, with opportunities to share, off load and review how things are going.

4 Organise workshops on particular issues, which could act as a supplement to themes covered in the course.

Running order

- **Off-load time**
- **Storytelling and listening**
  Parents' stories

This time the stories come from within the group. What have they gained from the course? What have been really important moments for them?

■ **Beginning to dream**

What might my future and that of my child look like?

■ **Something funny**

The funniest thing on the course

■ **Feelings check**

A different view of myself

This is a good exercise in building self-esteem. Working in small groups you're asking parents to think about the sort of skills and abilities they've developed because of being the parent of a child with special needs, for example staying calm in crisis situation, being accepting and patient. Ask parents to complete **Handout 28** A different view of myself, asking themselves the questions:

How do I feel about me now?

How have I changed?

Who have I become?

■ **Practical action**

A different view of my child: What do I want to say to my child?

Using **Handout 29** A different view of my child ask the parents to write down how they feel about their child with special needs. Some parents find this helpful to be written in the form of a letter, even if it is unlikely that the child will be able to read the letter.

Afterwards give those who wish to the opportunity to read out loud what they have written.

■ **Something to learn**

Ways Through (3)

Support ideas – Support groups

Circle of support

Continuing the discussion about support from last week, give a short presentation on the benefits of support groups and an explanation about what circles of support are.

■ **Practical action**

What are you going to do about support after the group is finished?

■ **Something to reflect**

Overview of the course

The good, the bad and the ugly – Have a frank and honest discussion about what parents liked, what they didn't understand and what should definitely be dropped if the course is repeated.

■ Looking after yourself

Review activities for the last time

Refer to written sheets again and in small groups each parent should plan their day or half a day for themselves.

■ Expressing appreciation and ending

Celebration – People I've met along the way

This is the group's opportunity to say what they've learnt from each other and what they've enjoyed about being in the group as opposed to the course content.

Bibliography

Ackerley, M. S. (1984) 'Developmental changes in families with autistic children: a parent's perspective', in Schopler, E. and Mesibov, G. B. (eds) *The Effects of Autism on the Family*. New York: Plenum Press.

Alvarez, A. and Reid, S. (1999) *Autism and Personality*. London: Routledge.

Armstrong, T. (1995) *The Myth of the ADD Child*. New York: Plume Books.

Beresford, B. (1994) *Positively Parents: Caring for a severely disabled child*. London: Social Policy Research Unit, HMSO.

Brazelton, T. B. and Cramer, B. G. (1990) *The Earliest Relationship: Parents, infants and the drama of early attachment*. Reading, MA: Addison Wesley Longman.

Bristol, M. M. (1984) 'Family resources and successful adaptation to autistic children', in Schopler, E. and Mesibov, G. B. (eds) *The Effects of Autism on the Family*. New York: Plenum Press.

Carpenter, B. (ed.) (1997) *Families in Context: Emerging trends in family support and early intervention*. London: David Fulton Publishers.

Carpenter, S. and Carpenter, B. (1997) 'Working with families', in Carpenter, B. (ed.) *Families in Context: Emerging trends in family support and early intervention*. London: David Fulton Publishers.

Carpenter, B. and Herbert, E. (1997) 'Fathers – Are we meeting their needs?', in Carpenter, B. (ed.) *Families in Context: Emerging trends in family support and early intervention*. London: David Fulton Publishers.

Chamba, R., Waquar Ahmed and Hirst, M. *et al.* (1999) *On the Edge: Minority ethnic families caring for a severely disabled child*. London: The Policy Press.

Clements, J. and Zarkowska, E. (2000) *Behavioural Concerns and Autistic Spectrum Disorders*. London: Jessica Kingsley.

Cowen, A. (2002) *Taking Care*. York: The Family Fund Trust.

Coyne Cutler, B. (1984) 'The parent as trainer of professionals: attitudes and acceptance', in Schopler, E. and Mesibov, G. B. (eds) *The Effects of Autism on the Family*. New York: Plenum Press.

Curtis, J. (2002) *Does Your Child Have a Hidden Disability?* London: Hodder & Stoughton.

Darley, S., Porter, J., Wemer, J. and Eberty, H. (2002) 'Families tell us what makes them strong', *The Exceptional Parent, Boston* **32**(12), 34–7.

Department for Education and Skills (DfES) (2001) *SEN Code of Practice for the Identification and Assessment of Pupils with Special Educational Needs*. London: DfES.

Department of Health (1999) *Quality Protects: Disabled children, numbers and categories and families*. London: HMSO.

Dobson, S. and Middleton, B. (1998) *Paying to Care: The cost of childhood disability*. York: Joseph Rowntree Foundation and York Publishing Services.

Donnellan, A., Lavigna, G. W., Negri-Shoult, N. and Fassbender, L. (1988) *Progress Without Punishment: Effective approaches for learners with behaviour problems*. New York: Teachers' College Press.

Faber, A. and Mazlish, E. (2001) *How to Talk so Kids will Listen and Listen so Kids will Talk*. London: Piccadily Press.

Falvey, M. A., Forest, M., Pierpoint, J. and Rosenburg, R. L. (1997) *All My Life's a Circle: Using the tools, circles, maps and paths*. Toronto, Canada: Inclusion Press.

Furlong, F. (1998) 'Self-esteem and the dyspraxic child', in Hunt, P. (ed.) *Praxis Makes Perfect*. Hitchin, Herts: Dyspraxia Foundation.

Garland, C. (1991) 'External disasters and the internal world: an approach to understanding survivors', in Holmes, J. (ed.) *Handbook in Psychotherapy for Psychiatrists*. London: Routledge.

Green, C. and Chee, K. (1997) *Understanding ADHD*. London: Vermillion Press.

Greenspan, S. L. and Wieder, S. (1998) *The Child with Special Needs: Encouraging intellectual and emotional growth*. Reading, MA: Addison Wesley Longman.

Hautamaki, A. (1997) 'Mothers – stress, stressors and strain outcomes of a cross Nordic study', in Carpenter, C. (ed.) *Families In Context: Emerging trends in family support and early intervention*, 31–50. London: David Fulton Publishers.

Hobson, R. P. (1997) *Autism and the Development of Mind*. London: Psychology Press.

Ives, M. and Munro, N. (2002) *Caring for a Child with Autism: A practical guide for parents*. London: Jessica Kingsley Publishers.

Jordan, R. (2001) *Autism with Severe Learning Difficulties*. London: Souvenir Press.

Kollberg, E., Hautamaki, A. and Heiberg, A. *et al.* (1990) *Families of Children with Disabilities in the Nordic Countries*. Place of publication: Nordic School of Public Health.

Kozlof, M. A. (1984) 'A training program for families of children with autism: responding to family needs', in Schopler, E. and Mesibov, G. (eds) *The Effects of Autism on the Family*. New York: Plenum Press.

Lamb, M. (1990) 'Fathers of exceptional children', in Seligman, M. (ed.) *The Family with a Handicapped Child: Understanding and treatment*, 2nd edn. New York: Allyn and Bacon.

Lazarus, R. S. and Folkman, S. (1984) 'Coping and adaption', in Gentry, W. D. (ed.) *Handbook of Behavioural Medicine*. New York: The Guildford Press.

Marchant, R. and Gordon, R. (2001) *Two-way Street: Communicating with disabled children and young people*. London: NSPCC and Joseph Rowntree Foundation.

Marcus, L. M. (1984) 'Coping with burnout', in Schopler, E. and Mesibov, G. (eds) *The Effects of Autism on the Family*. New York: Plenum Press.

Mason, M. (2000) *Incurably Human*. London: Working Press.

McCloughry, R. and Morris, W. (2002) *Making a World of Difference – Christian reflections on disability*. London: Hodder & Stoughton.

McCubbin, H. and Patterson, J. 'Broadening the scope of family strengths,' in Stinner, N. *et al*. *Family Strengths in Roots of well-being*. Lincoln NE: University of Nebraska Press.

McCubbin, H. and Patterson, J. (1982) 'Family Adoption to Crises', in McCubbin, H. Cauble, A. and Patterson, J. (eds) *Family Stress, Coping and Social Support*. Springfield, Illinois: C. C. Thomas.

Meyer, D. (1995) *Uncommon Fathers Reflections on Raising a Child with a Disability*. Bethesda, MD: Woodbine House.

Meyer, D. J. and Vadasy, P. F. (1994) *Sibshops: Workshops for siblings of children with special needs*. Baltimore: Paul H. Brookes Publishing.

Miller, A. C. *et al*. (1992) 'Stress, appraisal and coping in mothers of disabled and non-disabled children', *Journal of Pediatric Psychology* **17**, 587–605.

Minuchin, S. (1974) *Families and Family Therapy*. Cambridge: Harvard University Press.

Naseef, R. A. (2001) *Special Children Challenged Parents*, revised edn. Baltimore: Paul H. Brookes Publishing.

O'Brien, J. and O'Brien, C. L. (eds) (1998) *A Little Book About Person Centred Planning*. Toronto, Canada: Inclusion Press.

O'Brien, J., O'Brien, C. L. and Jacobs, G. *Celebrating the Ordinary: The emergence of options in community living as a thoughtful organisation*. Toronto, Canada: Inclusion Press.

Oldman, C. and Beresford, B. (1998) *Homes Unfit for Children: Housing disabled children and their families*. Place of publication: Policy Press.

Osherson, S. (1992) *Wrestling with Love: How men struggle with intimacy with women, children, parents and each other*. New York: Fawcett Columbine.

Pearlman, L. A. (date) *Traumatic Loss*. Massachusetts: Trauma Research, Education and Training Institute, University of Massachusetts.

Pierpoint, J. and Forest, M. (1998) 'The ethics of MAPS and PATHS', in O'Brien, J. and O'Brien, C. L. (eds) *A Little Book About Person Centred Planning*. Toronto, Canada: Inclusion Press.

Portwood, M. (1999) *Developmental Dyspraxia: Identification and Intervention – A manual for parents and professionals*, 2nd edn. London: David Fulton Publishers.

Puescel, S. M. and Bernier, J. C. (1984) 'The professional's role as advocate', in Schopler, E. and Mesibov, G. (eds) *The Effects of Autism on the Family*. New York: Plenum Press.

Quartley, B. and Rae, T. (2001) *Developing Parenting Skills, Confidence and Self-esteem*. Bristol: Lucky Duck Publishing.

Rosenburg, M. B. (1999) *Nonviolent Communication*. Encinitas, CA: PuddleDancer Press.

Schopler, E. and Mesibov, G. (eds) (1984) *The Effects of Autism on the Family*. New York: Plenum Press.

Seligman, M. and Darling, R. B. (1989) *Ordinary Families, Special Children: A systems approach to childhood disability*. New York: The Gulliford Press.

Small, M. W. (1998) 'After the plan', in O'Brien, J. and O'Brien, C. L. (eds) *A Little Book About Person Centred Planning*. Toronto, Canada: Inclusion Press.

Small, M. W. (1998) 'Revisiting choice', in O'Brien, J. and O'Brien, C. L. (eds) *A Little Book About Person Centred Planning*. Toronto, Canada: Inclusion Press.

Smith, C. (1997) *Developing Parenting Programmes*. London: National Bureau Enterprises.

Snow, J. (1998) 'The power in vulnerability', in O'Brien, J. and O'Brien, C. L. (eds) *A Little Book about Person Centred Planning*. Toronto, Canada: Inclusion Press.

Staub, E. and Pearlman, L. A. (2001) 'Creating a Path to Healing and Reconciliation after Genocide and other Collective Violence' from the book *Forgiveness and Reconciliation* (2001) by Helmick, R. G., Peterson, S. J. and Peterson, R. L., Radnor, PA: Templeton Foundation Press. Trauma Research, Education and Training Institute, University of Massachusetts.

Staudacher, C. (1991) *Men and Grief: A man's guide to recovering from the death of a loved one*. Oakland, CA: New Harbinger Publications.

Stobbs, P. and Rieser, R. (2002) *Making It Work – Removing disability discrimination – Are you ready?* Kings Langley, Herts: Direct Binders and Print.

Stock Whitaker, D. (1995) *Using Groups to Help People*. London: Routledge.

Street, E. (1998) 'Standing on your head: coping with the behavioural problems of children with developmental disorders', in Hunt, P. (ed.) *Praxis Makes Perfect*, 2nd edn. Hitchin, Herts: Dyspraxia Foundation.

Sullivan, R. C. (1979) 'Siblings of autistic children', *Journal of Autism and Developmental Disorders* **9**, 287–98.

Tessler, L. (1995) 'Self-esteem and the child with dyslexia', *Perspectives* (Orton Dyslexia Society) **21**, 3.

Trevarthen, C., Aitken, K., Papoudi, D. and Robarts, J. (1996) *Children with Autism: Diagnosis and intervention to meet their needs*. London: Jessica Kingsley.

Wheal, A. with Emson, G. (2002) *The Family Support Handbook*. Lyme Regis: Russel House Publishing.

Williams, D. (1996) *Autism: An inside out approach*. London: Jessica Kingsley.

Wolf, L., Noh, S., Firman, S. and Speechley, M. (1989) 'Psychological effects of parenting stress on parents of autistic children', *Journal Of Autism and Developmental Disorders* **19**, 1.

Legislation

Carers and Disabled Children Act 2000. London: HMSO.

Children Act 1989. London: HMSO.

Children (Northern Ireland) Order 1995. London: HMSO.

Children (Scotland) Act 1995. London: HMSO.

Education (Special Educational Needs Code of Practice) (England) Order 2001. London: HMSO.

Health and Personal Social Services (Northern Ireland) Order 1991. London: HMSO.

National Health Service (NHS) and Community Care Act 1990. London: HMSO.

Special Educational Needs and Disability Act 2001. London: HMSO.

APPENDIX: Handouts for group work

Handout 1 Course content

Course content

Session 1:   Introduction

Session 2:   Beginnings

Session 3:   Building up support

Session 4:   Communication and relationship building

Session 5:   Behaviour

Session 6:   Stress

Session 7:   Facing the feelings

Session 8:   Families

Session 9:   Hope

Session 10: Facing the future

Handout 2 Listening

Listening

is more than just hearing words.

The person you're listening to needs:

- your undivided attention
- your time
- your eye contact
- your acceptance
- your interest
- your emotional connection.

The person does not need:

- your advice
- your solutions
- your stories.

You need to think about:

- your body language
- your facial expression
- the feelings behind the person's words
- being aware of your emotions so you can connect
- how to summarise and reflect back what you've heard.

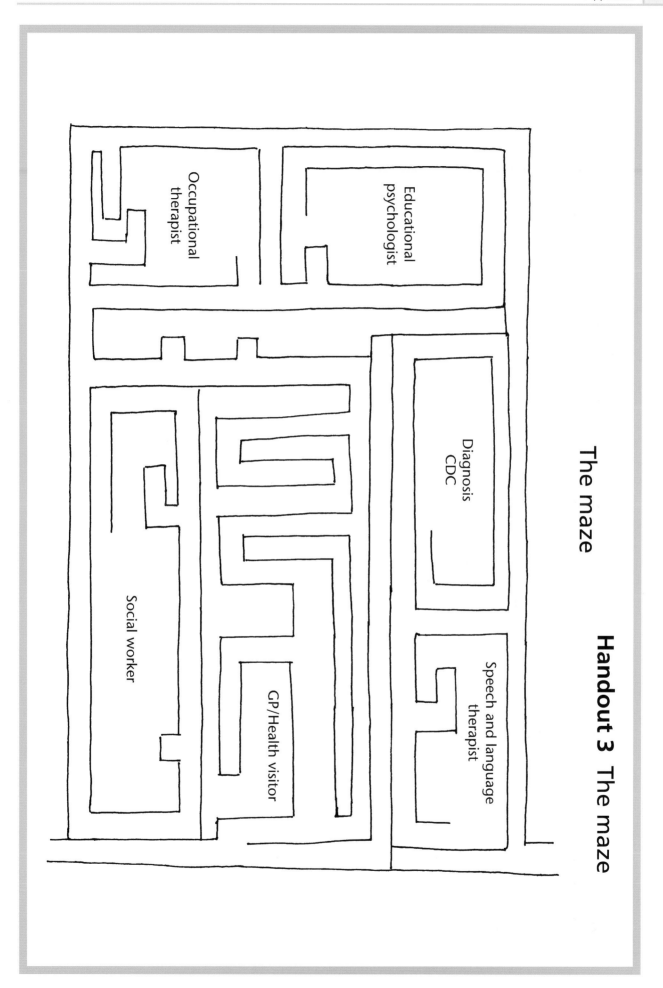

The maze

Handout 3 The maze

Handout 4 Social Model of disability

Social Model of disability

These definitions have been adapted from Micheline Mason's book *Incurably Human* (Mason 2000: 60).

- IMPAIRMENT: characteristic or feature within a person which is long term and may be the result of disease, injury or congenital condition and may:

  - affect that person's appearance in a way that is not acceptable to society;

  - affect that person's mind or body either because of, or regardless of, society;

  - affect pain and fatigue levels;

  - affect communication and memory.

- LEARNING DIFFICULTIES: implies difficulties that can be overcome with the right support. Also implies there is still an individual there who has potential in his or her own right.

- DISABILITY: disadvantage and restriction of activity caused by the systems and practices in society which exclude people with impairments.

Handout 5 The education process

The education process

School Action

When a class teacher notices that a child has special educational needs there will be a meeting between the parent, class teacher and the special educational needs co-ordinator (SENCO). At this stage, what they are looking for is information about your child, his strengths and weaknesses. Any observations you have are really important. They may want to contact other professionals, such as your health visitor, who have already had contact with him. But they will only do that with your permission.

After this meeting, using all the information, the SENCO will:

- put together an Individual Education Plan (IEP).

- set up, with the class teacher, some extra support for your child additional to and different from what he would normally expect to get in the classroom. It might include: special equipment, small groups focusing on a subject, one-to-one support, and training for staff in how best to support your child.

- arrange regular meetings to review your child's progress.

School Action Plus

If your child's special educational needs carry on causing concern, it's likely that at one of the regular meetings that take place, it will be decided that more support is needed. The class teacher and SENCO will refer to outside agencies so that outside specialists can suggest other options. Such specialists include:

educational psychologists, specialist learning support teachers from the Education Department, occupational therapists or speech therapists.

First of all the specialist will assess the child in a particular area. Often, the specialist will come to the school to observe your child in his classroom and have some separate one-to-one time with him. Sometimes you will be asked to take your child to an assessment centre for an appointment.

From this assessment, the specialist will write a report with suggestions and there will be a meeting with him or her, the class teacher and you to put a plan into place. From this meeting several things may happen:

- There may be a diagnosis, although what is more likely is that a diagnosis process is started where you and your child are asked to attend a series of appointments.

- There is likely to be advice to teachers on how to work with your child.

- There may be new equipment, teaching and learning materials.

- There may be extra teaching support for your child.

- There may be new IT software introduced at school for your child.

Statutory Assessment

If as a parent you do feel that under School Action Plus your child is not making enough progress ask the school to make a request to the local education authority (LEA) for a Statutory Assessment. As soon as the LEA receives a request there is a 26 week time limit. The first stage is that the LEA decides whether an assessment is necessary, this takes six weeks. The authority will look for evidence from the school, parents and other professionals about the child's learning difficulties. At this point, as a parent, you can write your own report, ask the LEA to approach other professionals about your child and ask to be invited to any meetings to discuss your child. If after six weeks the LEA agrees to a Statutory Assessment, they will tell you, the parents, who is going to conduct the assessments on the child. This does not usually take more than ten weeks.

Following the assessment if it is decided that there is no Statement of special educational needs, the LEA must inform the parents and include information about how to appeal. A 'Note in Lieu' may be offered. However, if it is decided a Statement of special educational needs will be granted, the LEA will inform the parents and include the proposed Statement.

The Statement

The Statement is in six parts:

1 Introduction – names and addresses of parent and child and other details

2 Special educational needs – all the child's special educational needs

3 Special educational provision – the special educational help the child must be provided with

4 Place – the name of the school or other place where the child must be educated

5 Non-educational needs – the child's non-educational difficulties

6 Non-educational provision – the non-educational help that should be provided for the child.

Handout 6 Education terms

Education terms

Annual Review

The review of a Statement of special educational needs which an LEA must make within 12 months of making the Statement.

Education Welfare Officer

Person employed by the LEA to help parents make sure their children attend school. In some areas called Education Social Workers.

Foundation Stage

Begins when children reach three years old and continues until the end of their reception year.

Graduated approach

Way of acting and intervening in schools to help children with special needs. This recognises that there is a range of special needs and that some children will need specialist help from outside.

Individual Education Plan (IEP)

This is a working document about the child recording key short-term targets and strategies for him that are different from and additional to those in place for the rest of his class.

Learning mentors

School staff who work with teaching staff to work out and identify those children who need extra help to overcome barriers to learning inside and outside the school.

Learning Support Assistants (LSAs)

Assistants who provide in-school support for children with special needs. An LSA will normally work with a particular child or group of children providing close support. They will also help the teacher in charge of teaching the child.

Named LEA Officer

The person from the LEA who co-ordinates and acts as a bridge between the LEA and parents over all the arrangements for Statutory Assessments and Statements. When an LEA lets a parent know that they are going to make a Statutory Assessment for the child, they must let the parent know who the Named Officer is.

National Curriculum

Sets out what children will learn at school; what should be taught and targets for learning. It also sets out how a child's performance will be assessed and reported.

National Curriculum Inclusion Statement

Statement in the National Curriculum about inclusion. It details principles that must be followed to make sure a child has a chance to succeed, whatever their needs and their barriers to learning.

Note in Lieu

When an LEA decide not to make a Statement they may issue a 'Note in Lieu' to the child's parents. The note should describe the child's special educational needs, explain why a Statement has not been issued and make recommendations about suitable provision for the child. All the advice received during the child's Statutory Assessment should be attached to it.

Pupil Referral Unit

Any school maintained by an LEA which is organised to provide an education for children who do not otherwise receive an education due to exclusion, illness or another reason.

SEN co-ordinator (SENCO)

School member of staff who has responsibility for co-ordinating special educational needs provision within that school. Who does this job varies from school to school. In smaller schools, it may be the head teacher or deputy, larger schools may have an SEN co-ordinating team.

SEN Tribunal

An independent body set up under the Education Act of 1996 to settle appeals by parents against LEA decisions on assessments and Statements. The Tribunal's decision will be compulsory on both sides.

Handout 7 Benefits

Benefits

Benefits you may be able to claim if you are caring for a disabled child include:

- Disability Living Allowance (DLA)

- Carer's Allowance (CA)

- Council Tax reductions (if your house has been specially adapted because of your child's disability)

- Road Tax exemption (if your child gets the higher rate mobility component of DLA)

- Help with NHS costs (if you have a low income)

- Help with hospital fares for treatment or visiting a child in hospital (if you have a low income)

- If you receive Income Support you should also receive:

  - Disabled Child Premium (if your child gets DLA)
  - Carer Premium (if you qualify for CA)
  - Community Care Grant

Handout 8 Signposts

Signposts

Who does what?

Social Services Departments (England and Wales)

Social Service Trusts (Northern Ireland)

Social Work Departments (Scotland)

Services that should be available:

- Assessment on needs, planning child care plans and regulation of services
- Assessment of carer's needs
- Social work and counselling
- Family aide
- Short-term respite care
- Occupational therapy
- Direct Payments
- Equipment such as ramps, special cutlery etc.
- Adaptations to housing – social services should liaise with housing about grants available
- Interpreter and translating
- Advocacy and representation for children and parents to help represent their views
- Benefits advice
- Information about services
- Blue badge scheme
- Information on playgroups, nurseries and childminders

Differences in regions: In Scotland social services have to make provision for brothers and sisters of children with a disability.

The Health Service

Services that should be available:

- Family doctor (GP)
- Hospital specialists (referred by your GP)
- Health visitors
- Child Development Centres or Children's Centres (names may vary) where a team of people, including paediatricians, physiotherapists, speech and language therapists, work together to assess a child's special needs. These services vary, in rural areas it may be a home-based service.
- Community care nurses (for people with learning difficulties)
- Continence services – free nappies
- Wheelchairs and buggies through the wheelchair centre
- Callipers, crutches and other mobility equipment

Education Departments (England, Wales and Scotland)
Education and Library Boards (Northern Ireland)

Services that should be available:

- Home-based learning programme (for example, Portage)
- Assessment of children with special educational needs from the age of two years
- Nursery schooling
- Special educational provision in mainstream or special school. This may be: pupil support assistant help, individualised special help such as speech and language therapy, mid-day supervision etc.
- Re-assessment

- Annual Review of child's Statement to which parents should be invited

- Schooling up to the age of 19 if needed and funding for further education or local college.

Differences in regions: In Scotland schooling is only offered up to the age of 18.

Department for Work and Pensions (formerly the Benefits Agency) – England, Scotland and Wales

Department for Social Development (Benefits Agency) – Northern Ireland

Same benefit system for all (see **Handout 7** Benefits for details).

Voluntary organisations

Services that should be available:

- Information about local services for disabled children, benefits and other information

- Information about different impairments

- Practical help such as special toy libraries, playschemes and sitting services

- Contact with other parents through support groups

How do I get in touch with them?

- Look in your local phone book for details of: local council, unitary authority or county council to find addresses and phone numbers for social services and education departments. Ask for Disabled Children's Team (social services) and Special Education (education departments).

- For health services, ask your GP to refer you.

- Any health professional can refer you to your local wheelchair centre.

- Continence adviser can be contacted direct.

- Voluntary organisations can be contacted via: Citizen's Advice Bureau, library, disability group or local Council for Voluntary Service (CVS)

This information is adapted from *Taking Care* by Alison Cowen (2002).

What people do

Community paediatric nurse

Can help with practical tasks involving nursing at home.

Health visitor

Can advise on practical ways of coping and caring for your child on day-to-day matters.

Occupational therapist

Can support you in helping your child manage daily tasks, such as dressing and going to the toilet. They also give advice on and can arrange for you to be supplied with aids, equipment and adaptations to your home which can make life easier for you and your child.

Physiotherapist

Can provide treatment and advice to help relieve pain and increase mobility.

Community psychiatric nurse

Can give you advice if your child has mental health problems and sometimes give your child medication.

Speech therapist

Helps children who have speech, language and communication disorders.

Continence adviser

Can give you practical help if your child is incontinent.

Community paediatrician

Will assess and monitor your child's developmental needs and organise therapy and services where appropriate.

Handout 9 The communication process

The communication process

Age of child	The way they communicate	What they learn	What can be different for children with special needs
Young babies 0–6 months	■ Eye contact ■ Turn-taking ■ Sharing of emotions ■ Learning cause and effect	■ How to take a turn in a human 'conversation' ■ The beginning of: Self-awareness Emotional connection with others	■ Do not give the eye-contact trigger, so don't experience human conversations ■ Difficulties in their relationship with parent – no shared emotion; hard to bond
Older babies 6–12 months	■ Joint regard ■ Shared attention	■ Learns to concentrate on the same thing as his parent ■ Begins to understand what words mean	■ Without eye contact joint regard and shared attention are not possible ■ If a baby perceives things differently (you see a ball, he sees a shiny surface) this is going to have

(*continued*)

Age of child	The way they communicate	What they learn	What can be different for children with special needs
			a big effect on the way words are used
Young toddlers 1–2 years	■ Using a lot of words and starting to put them together in phrases and sentences ■ Understanding more of what is being said to them, e.g. words and simple phrases like, 'shoes on' ■ Are learning a great deal through playing with other children	■ Begins to learn how to have conversations ■ Experiences emotions, gains more understanding of them and begins to put names to them ■ Learns the effect he has on others	■ Often little or no language and poor understanding of language ■ Little learning of conversations and few opportunities to play with others ■ Find it hard to understand what they are doing or feeling ■ Find it hard to learn how their actions might affect others, or learn the language of play – social language
Older toddlers 2–5 years	■ Saying sentences and simple stories ■ Beginning to	■ Learning how to use complicated language	■ Not understanding conversations increasingly

Age of child	The way they communicate	What they learn	What can be different for children with special needs
	understand ideas such as 'bigger' and 'smaller' ■ Understanding more information	■ Learning how to process more than one item of information at the same time	causes all sorts of problems for them ■ Words are repeated parrot-fashion with little understanding of meaning (Echolalia)
School-age children	■ Mastering two-way conversations ■ Understanding abstract concepts ■ Beginning to make sense of double meanings in language ■ Able to conduct long and detailed exchanges of information	■ Learning the rules of a two-way conversation: understand gestures, tone and body language ■ Developing a good sense of humour ■ Understanding how to get on with people and negotiate relationships	■ Don't understand the rules of conversation; words used repetitively, it doesn't relate to the conversation, staying 'on-track' in a conversation is difficult ■ Find it hard to process long streams of words ■ Language is often understood literally

Handout 10 Ways of helping with communication

Ways of helping with communication

(1) General

- Have an attitude of acceptance and understanding
- Have an open attitude that wants to give and respond
- Rediscover what we enjoy about our child
- Have respectful attitude for a child's struggle
- Look at our style of communication
- Be honest about your feelings
- Find a way of expressing feeling without doing damage
- Find a way where we feel good about ourselves
- Remember that communication is more than words
- Time, space and silence
- Active listening
- Avoid escalation
- Follow the child's lead

(2) For children who use language

- Be clear
- Describe what you see
- Don't ask too many questions
- Use different language. For example, say:

- *'I feel'* then say how you feel
- *'When'* then say what happens
- *'Because'* then say why it affected you
- *'What are we going to do about it?'*

(3) For children who use other forms of communication

- Keep language simple
- Use speech systems and early intervention therapies
- Build up self-awareness for children of what they want
- Act dumb rather than anticipating your child's needs
- Celebrate communication with enthusiasm and make it interesting

Handout 11 Communication alternatives

Communication alternatives

Communication aids

British Sign Language (BSL)

BSL is the visual language of the deaf community. It has its own structure, grammar and word order.

For more information: The National Deaf Children's Society

Blissymbolics

Bliss is a symbol system, first used for children with physical impairments. Children access it from a book, board or a range of computer systems. It has abstract symbols and a wide-ranging vocabulary.

For more information: Blissymbol Communication UK

Makaton Language Programme

This is designed for children with communication, language and literacy difficulties and uses a small core of words taken from everyday life which can be added to.

For more information: Makaton Vocabulary Development Project

Objects of Reference

Real objects are used to represent activities, concepts or people. Children may use them in a bag or box, carried around with them to express basic needs. Also they can be used as an object calendar or for the beginning and end of an activity.

For more information: Sense

PECS (Picture Exchange Communication System)

PECS starts with communication for things the child wants. It builds to six phases ranging from single picture symbols to complex sentences where children comment on how they feel.

For more information: Pyramid Educational Consultants UK Ltd

Signalong

This is a sign vocabulary based on BSL. It is designed for children with learning and communication difficulties. The signs are used with speech.

For more information: The Signalong Group

TEACCH

This is a way of adults communicating with children using the same symbols as PECS. It can be used in pictorial timetables, to help children predict what is going to happen next and to move from one activity to another.

For more information: The Training Services Department of the National Autistic Society

Therapies based on communication

Music Assisted Communication

Music responds to the child's actions in a structured interaction. Children often appreciate the structure of music whereas they have more difficulties with understanding the spoken word.

For more information: see APMT.

The Hanen Method

This helps parents build up and sustain early relationships with their children. Parents come together in groups in understanding their children and ways of working with them.

For more information: see Hanen UK

The Option Approach

The approach is to re-learn basic social interactions by slowing them down to the point that the child gets a pleasurable response from the experience and then building from there. It is a home-based programme.

For more information: see the Options Institute

Handout 12 Iceberg model

Iceberg model

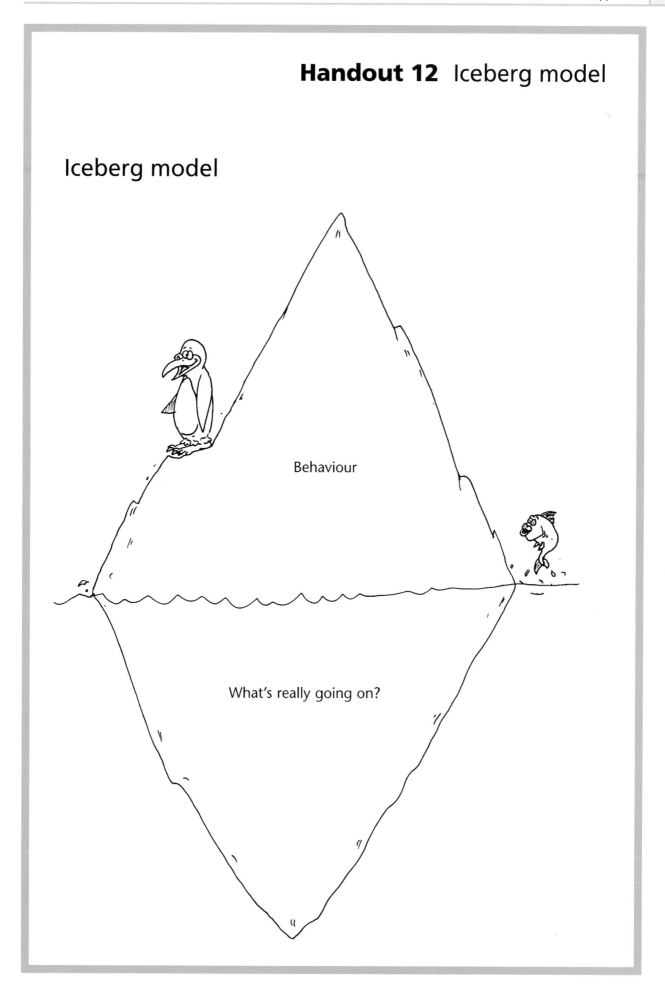

Behaviour

What's really going on?

Handout 13 Stimuli/belief/response

Stimuli/belief/response

Stimuli
What's going on out there

Belief
What's going on in here

Response
What I'm going to do

Handout 14 Belief systems

Belief systems

What I believe about myself that is unhelpful:

■ 'I'm a useless parent and that there is nothing I can do that will change anything.'

■ 'I daren't change anything at home, if I do all hell will break loose.'

■ 'The problem is this child's behaviour. I'm going to punish him so badly, he won't know what's hit him.'

■ 'This child is deliberately trying to hurt me.'

■ 'This child is ruining my life; my life is a total nightmare.'

What I believe about myself that is helpful:

■ 'I am a good parent, I do love my child and I can make a difference.'

■ 'I've started to realise that I am the expert where my child is concerned.'

Handout 15 Behaviour toolkit

Behaviour toolkit

General

- Looking after yourself

- Have a home atmosphere of nurture

- Be enthusiastic and excited when they do what we want

- Be flexible

- Anticipate what might happen

- Routines and rituals

- Rewards

- Be consistent and clear

- Avoid big angry scenes

- Have natural and simple consequences

- Use time out

- Use relaxation techniques

- Look at the child's diet

- Reduce the background sensory information at home

- Reduce the amount of TV, video or PlayStation they see

Specific ideas for children with severe or moderate learning or communication difficulties

- Introduce a different behaviour

- Diversion

- Breaking down a task

- Prompting

Specific ideas for children with mild learning and communication difficulties and ADHD disorders

- Teach self-talk skills

- Teach problem solving

- Help your child to be resilient

- Encourage children's creativity

Handout 16 Behaviour stressbusting

Behaviour stressbusting

- **Where do I start?**

  Don't try and deal with everything at once but look at which behaviour is causing you and your family the most stress. If that doesn't narrow it down consider the following:

  - *Is the behaviour dangerous to herself or others?*
  - *Does the behaviour really reduce the quality of people's lives?*
  - *Does the behaviour restrict the quality of the child's life? (e.g. child refuses to go out)*
  - *Is the behaviour very destructive?*
  - *Is her behaviour unacceptable in society when she goes out?*

  When you've decided, ask yourself what might be the trigger for this behaviour.

- **What might be the trigger for this behaviour?**

  The trigger may be:

  - Place
  - Sound
  - People
  - Changes in routine
  - Illness
  - Diet
  - External stress in the family.

- **How does it make you feel when the behaviour happens?**

  Guilt, fear, deep hurt, anger, disappointment, embarrassment and/or shame?

- **How do you respond?**

  Does it completely freeze you up? Do you over-react?

- **What is the belief system behind this response?**

  What do you believe about yourself as a parent when this behaviour happens?

- **Are there any practical solutions to this behaviour?**

- **Can you avoid the issue that triggers it?**

- **How can you change your belief systems?**

  For example, 'I am doing the best I can in very difficult circumstances.'

- **What tools can I use from my behaviour toolkit?**

Handout 17 Stress

Stress

Handout 18 Post-traumatic stress disorder

Post-traumatic stress disorder

Feelings

Emotional numbness

Blankness, not feeling anything

Not being able to cope with everyday situations

Guilt

Tears

'Mood swings': irritability, anger, suspicion and fear

Physical reactions

Problems with sleeping

Easily startled

Having trouble concentrating

Actions

Isolate yourself

Find it harder to make decisions or remember things

Handout 19 'Perfect' parent and child

'Perfect' parent and child

Handout 20 Stressbusting kit

Stressbusting kit

- See looking after yourself as a priority

- Become visible, ask for help

- Be gentle and kind to yourself

- Stop seeing letting feelings out as a weakness

- Make connections with physical and emotional feelings

- Get more information

- 'Loving neglect'

- Let go of the expectations and pressures of performance-led parenting

Handout 21 Cycle of emotions

Cycle of emotions

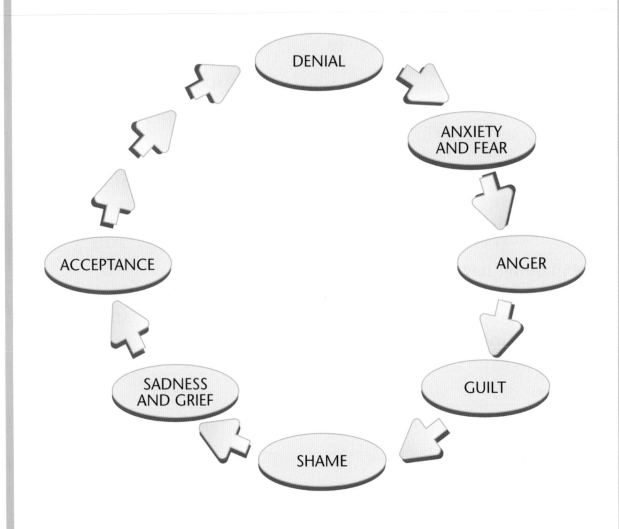

Feelings list

Relaxed	Pleased
Broken hearted	Annoyed
Proud	Affectionate
Enthusiastic	Hopeful
Mellow	Inspired
Good humoured	Ashamed
Grateful	Exhausted
Happy	Bewildered
Distressed	Embarrassed
Refreshed	Animated
Afraid	Satisfied
Beat	Encouraged
Frustrated	Angry
Confused	Apprehensive
Puzzled	Troubled
Agitated	Detached
Energetic	Thankful
Despondent	Confident
Disquieted	Amused
Disappointed	Contented
Anguished	Fearful
Joyful	Despairing
Loving	Unhappy
Calm	Upbeat
Sad	Dejected
Cheerful	Pessimistic
Alive	Furious
Anxious	Guilty
Depressed	Weary
Sorrowful	Numb

Handout 23 Cycle of Behaviour

Cycle of Behaviour

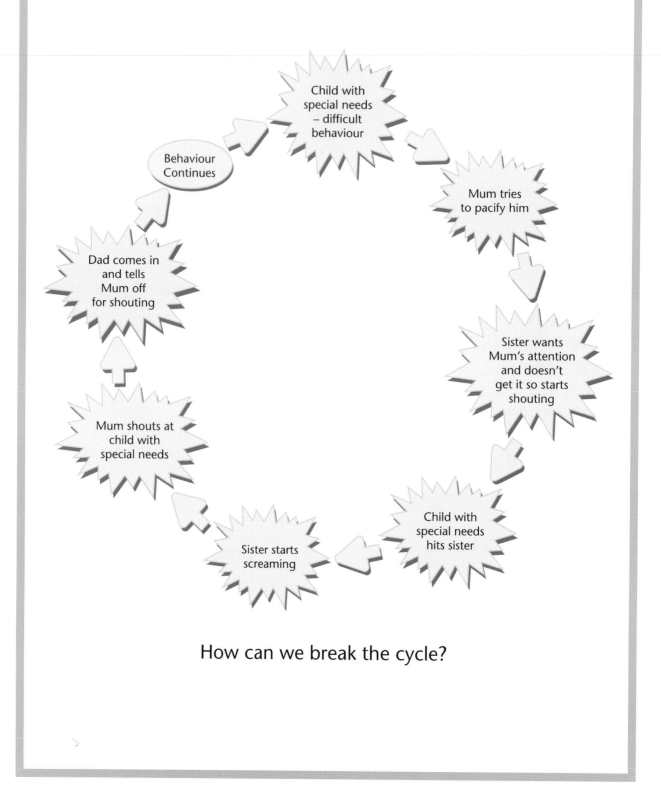

How can we break the cycle?

Handout 24 Problem solving

Problem solving

Questions to ask:

■ What is the problem?

■ Who is involved?

■ Who's problem is it?

■ What's been tried to resolve it?

Pause:

■ Listen to each other

■ Express how you feel

■ Accept that each other has a right to those feelings

Action:

■ Whose needs need meeting first?

■ List three possible options to solving the problem

■ Look for a solution which is a negotiated compromise

■ Remain calm!

Handout 25 Family moving-on kit

Family moving-on kit

Three key issues that help move a family on:

1   A family who works together.

Co-operate with each other, understand each other's needs, support and help each other and do things together as a family.

2   A family who are able to express feelings openly to each other.

There is encouragement at home to act openly and express their feelings directly.

3   A family who have a life outside the home.

Members of the family are actively involved in social and leisure activities outside the home with people outside their immediate family.

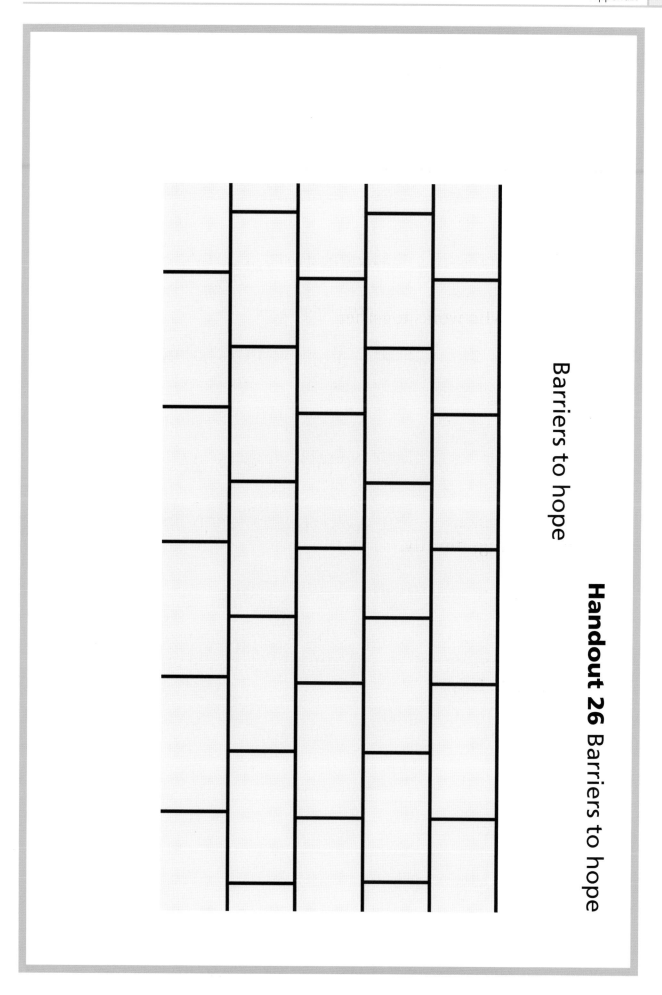

Barriers to hope

Handout 26 Barriers to hope

Handout 27 Relationship web

Relationship web

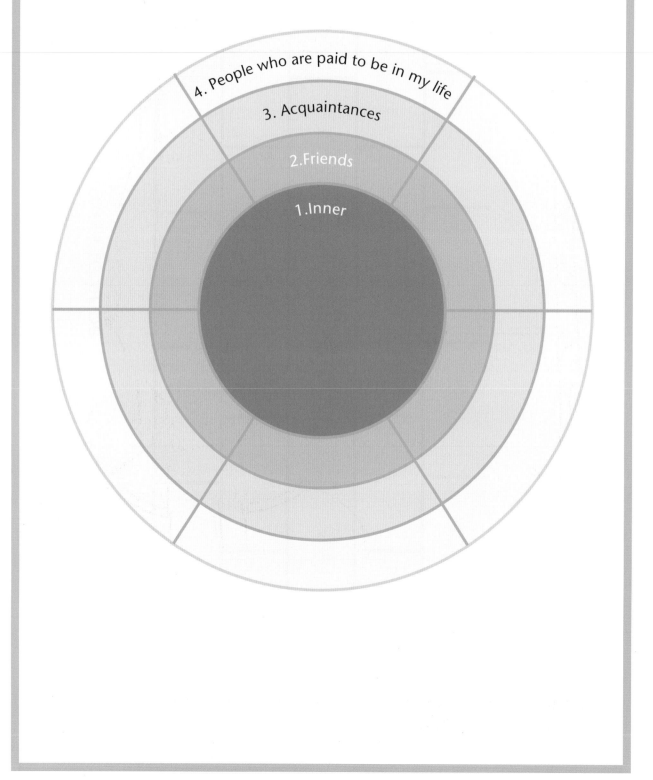

Handout 28 A different view of myself

A different view of myself

Write your thoughts on the mirror about how you have changed for the better.

Handout 29 A different view of my child

A different view of my child

Instead of	Look differently
Hyperactive	Energetic tactile learner
Learning disabled	Learning different
Autistic	Unique and fascinating view of the universe
Aggressive	Assertive
Plodding	Thorough
Lazy	Relaxed
Immature	In touch with the inner child
Dreamy	Imaginative
Irritable	Sensitive
Obsessive	Persistent
Impulsive	Spontaneous
Inattentive	Global thinker with a wide focus